# MUFFY VANDEI

## IDENTIFICATION & PRIC

### by Ann Gehlbach

Published by  Hobby House Press, Inc.
Grantsville, Maryland 21536

*This guide is dedicated to*
# Muffy®

Photography by North American Bear Company
See pages: Front Cover, 1, 4-6, 9, 13, 15, 18-23, 26, 33, 35, 37-44, 46, 48 (top), 49 (bottom), 51 (top), 52, 54 (top), 55 (top), 58 (top left & bottom), 60 (bottom), 62, 64 (top), 65, 66 (bottom), 71, 73 (bottom), 75, 79, 80-89, 91-96, Back Cover.
Photography by Ric Miracle
See pages: 3, 10-12, 14, 16-17, 24-25, 27-32, 34, 36, 39 (bottom), 42, 45, 47, 48 (bottom), 49 (top), 50, 51 (bottom), 53, 54 (bottom), 55 (bottom), 56-57, 58 (top right), 59, 60 (top), 61, 63, 64 (bottom), 66 (top), 67-70, 72, 73 (top), 74, 76-78, 90, 97-105.

*Front Cover:* Muffy **Butterfly**, First Club Edition. *See page 46 for more information.*
*Title Page:* Muffy **Rose**, Second Boxed Limited Edition. *See page 63 for more information.*
*Back Cover:* VanderBear Family dressed in old-fashioned nightwear: **Cornelius, Alice, Muffy, Fuzzy, Fluffy.** *See page 34 for more information.*

## BIOGRAPHY:

ANN GEHLBACH lives in Sarasota, Florida with her husband Don. They have been collecting bears for over 10 years. Ann was bitten by the "Muffy Bug" about 8 years ago, when she purchased her first Muffy for her daughter's Christmas present. She has been an avid collector ever since. Five years ago their bear collection outgrew their home and Ann and Don opened Village Bears & Collectibles on Siesta Key, Florida. Soon, their daughter, who is also a collector, joined them as the shop manager. Frustrated at being unable to answer customers' many questions about Muffy, Ann decided to compile a VanderBear history as a reference guide for herself. That little project soon got out of hand and after three years of research, that original 3 page history had grown into a book! Ann has met hundreds of Muffy collectors in the past five years from all over the world. Many have become cherished friends and each one helped to write this guide to Muffy's life.....each day brought another phone call or an E-mail with a newly discovered variation. Through this experience, Ann has found that Muffy fanatics all have two things in common......a sense of humor and a devotion to Muffy. After all, who could not love a little seven inch bear who loves dressing up and has so much fun!

*I would like to thank the following for their help and support during the research of this Guide:*
- The Muffy® collectors who shared their knowledge and discoveries.
- The Muffy® fanatics on Prodigy® who managed to come up with another variation just when I thought I'd seen them all.
- Mychael Allen and Terry Swartout for photos from their collection.
- North American Bear Company®
- And special hugs to Laura Collins who always knew the answer or where to find it, no matter how ridiculous the question was!

*Muffy® Identification & Price Guide* is an independent study by the author, Ann Gehlbach, and published by Hobby House Press, Inc. The research and publication of this book were not sponsored in any way by the manufacturers of the bears, the bear costumes, and the bear accessories featured in this study. Photographs of the collectibles were from bears, costumes, or accessories belonging to Ann Gehlbach at the time the picture was taken unless otherwise credited.

The information as to the ownership pertains to documentary materials contemporary with the bear or bear's accessories. Ownership of the registered trademark, the trademark, or the copyright may have expired or been transferred to another owner.

In order to capture the greatest detail of the bears and accessories in the photographic process, the bears and accessories will appear a different size than in real life.

The values given within this book are intended as value guides rather than arbitrarily set prices. The values quoted are as accurate as possible but in the case of errors, typographical, clerical, or otherwise, the author and publisher assume no liability nor responsibility for any loss incurred by users of this book.

All fur trimmings on costumes is fake.

Additional copies of this book may be purchased at $19.95 (plus postage and handling) from
**Hobby House Press, Inc.**
1 Corporate Drive
Grantsville, Maryland 21536
**1-800-554-1447**
or from your favorite bookstore or dealer.

# TABLE OF CONTENTS

Life Is One Big Dress-Up ...................................................4

A Quick Guide to Muffy® and Her Family ....................7

The VanderBear Family® History ...............................9

The Muffy VanderBear® Club ...................................97

Muffy VanderBear®: The Bare Facts ........................99

Muffy® in the Spotlight ...........................................106

More Muffy® Trivia ................................................106

Glossary.................................................................109

Price Guide .............................................................110

How many Muffys do you see?

*Muffy*
*Muffy*
*Muffy*
*Muffy*
*Muffy*
*Muffy*
*Muffy*
*Muffy*
*Muffy*
*Muffy*
*Muffy*
*Muffy*
*Muffy*
*Muffy*
*ffy*
*ffy*
*ffy*
*ffy*
*ffy*
*ffy*
*Muffy*
*Muffy*
*Muffy*
*Muffy*

# Life is One

A bouncing little bundle of fuzz was delivered to VanderBear Manor in 1984. Wearing an eyelet trimmed christening gown, Muffy was welcomed as the littlest member of the VanderBear Family, and nothing's been the

same since. She keeps the whole family on the go, and that's just the way they like it. The family includes papa Cornelius, an inventor and philosopher-at-large; kind and cultured mama Alice; and brother and sister Fuzzy and Fluffy (they're twins, but to tell you the truth, they look nothing alike).

Where do the VanderBears live? Well, let's just say you can look for them in the State of Exaggeration. If you happen to drop in, they'll probably declare a holiday and throw you a party. They celebrate any and all holidays and occasions (including a few they've made up). The VanderBears love

# Big Dress Up

wearing the costumes and learning the customs of all the places they visit around the world.

Muffy has many friends, pets, and pals whom she has made during her young lifetime...like Oatsie, the one-trick pony; Lulu, a Scottish MacFluff (a rather rare breed of pup); and Purrlie, the calico kitten. But none can compare to her best friend and bosom bunny, the wild and glamorous Hoppy VanderHare, who accompanies the VanderBears on many of their adventures.

As you turn these pages, you will see that Muffy has an outfit for almost any occasion, because she believes that the best way to have an adventure is to dress for it. After all, as Muffy always says...

"Life is one big dress-up."

## The History of Muffy and the VanderBear Family

This excerpt appears in the front of the Muffy VanderBear® 1997 Spring Collection Catalog. Used with permission.

# HOW TO USE THIS GUIDE

Author Ann Gehlbach has researched each and every Muffy release to aid you in identification purposes. Arranged chronologically by year of release, the collection name, full descriptions of members costumes, and retirement dates are provided. Variations are categorized and an accompanying photograph captures the whimsical love of Muffy and her family. Keep in mind, that even though this guide has involved years of research and the help if many collectors, there will always be a different variation or another fact that is yet to be discovered. Just because it isn't listed, doesn't mean that it doesn't exist! Some collectors have also noticed differences in some tags that are sewn into Muffy's outfits, but since many of the early outfits did not have tags, documentation proved impossible.

Besides descriptions and variations, other helpful information is included. Hangtags for each Muffy are either described or featured in the photograph. Another common question that collectors ask — "How do I tell if a bear is factory dressed?" is answered in a special "The Bare Facts" section which includes exact wording of sewn-in tags and a few examples of outfits that came factory dressed on that particular Muffy. If that's not enough, test your Muffy knowledge in "More Muffy Trivia."

Enjoy this peek into Muffy's life!

# A QUICK GUIDE TO MUFFY AND HER FAMILY

## 1983 Issues
**Classic Velvet Family** (1983-1988)
  Cornelius • Alice • Fluffy • Fuzzy

## 1984
**Muffy Christening** (1984 —  )

## 1985
**Red Flannel Holiday Collection** (1985-1985)
  Cornelius • Alice • Fluffy • Fuzzy • Muffy

## 1986
**Muffy Valentine I** (1986-1989)
Cruisewear Collection (1986-1988, Muffy in 1991)
  Cornelius • Alice • Fluffy • Fuzzy • Muffy
**Muffy Witch, Halloween I** (1986-1988)
**Taffeta Holiday Collection** (1986-1986)
  Cornelius • Alice • Fluffy • Fuzzy • Muffy

## 1987
**A Day In the Country Collection** (1987-1989, Muffy in 1991)
  Cornelius • Alice • Fluffy • Fuzzy • Muffy
**Nutcracker Suite Collection** (1987-1987)
  Cornelius • Alice • Fluffy • Fuzzy • Muffy

## 1988
**Out of It In Africa** (1988-1991, Muffy in 1992)
  Cornelius • Alice • Fluffy • Fuzzy • Muffy
**Muffy Black Cat, Halloween II** (1988-1995)
**Furrier and Ives, The Skating Party** (1988-1988)
  Cornelius • Alice • Fluffy • Fuzzy• Muffy

## 1989
**Muffy Valentine II** (1989-1991)
**Muffy Bunny** (1989 —  )
**High Tea, The Tea Party Collection** (1989-1991, Muffy in 1992)
  Cornelius • Alice • Fluffy • Fuzzy • Muffy
**Muffy Pilgrim** (1989 —  )
**Tree Trimming Collection** (1989-1989)
  Cornelius • Alice • Fluffy • Fuzzy • Muffy, Scottie VanderDog
**Muffy Angel** (1989-1989)

## 1990
**Muffy Valentine III** (1990-1994)
**Muffy St. Patrick's Day** (1990 —  )
**Muffy Chick** (1990-1994)
**Muffy at the Beach** (1990 —  )
**Gibearny, an Impressionist Collection** (1990-1993)
  Cornelius • Alice • Fluffy • Fuzzy • Muffy

**Remembearances, A Wedding Collection** (1990-1991)
  Cornelius • Alice
**Back to School** (1990-1993)
  Muffy • Hoppy
**Sweet Dreams, the Victorian Sleepwear Collection** (1990-1992, Muffy in 1993)
  Cornelius • Alice • Fluffy • Fuzzy • Muffy
**Musical Soiree, The Purple Velvet Collection** (1990-1991, Muffy in 1992)
  Cornelius • Alice • Fluffy • Fuzzy • Muffy
**Muffy, Little Fir Tree** (1990-1990)

## 1991
**Mommy and Me, The Teacup Collection (1991-1994)**
  Alice • Muffy
**Easter Fantasy** (1991-1996)
  Muffy • Hoppy
**The Wild West, A Traveling Road Show** (1991-1994)
  Cornelius • Alice • Fluffy • Fuzzy • Muffy • Oatsie
**Paw De Deux** (1991 —  )
**The Fortune Tellers, Muffy, Hoppy** (1991 —  )
  Muffy Gypsy • Hoppy Genie
**The Ballet Recital** (1991-1994)
  Muffy • Hoppy
**Muffy SnowBear** (1991-1991)
**Bal Masque, The Legendary Party Collection** (1991-1992, Muffy, Hoppy, Oatsie in 1993)
  Cornelius • Alice • Fluffy • Fuzzy • Muffy • Hoppy • Oatsie
**Muffy Butterfly** (1991-1993) *(First Club Edition – Not available in stores)*
**Underthings** (1991 —  )
  Muffy • Hoppy

## 1992
**Down on the Farm** (1992 —  )
  Muffy • Farm Friends: Patti the Cow • Mary The Lamb • Rudy The Pig • Lucy the Goose • Webster the Duck
**Dutch Treat** (1992-1995)
  Muffy • Hoppy
**Cherry Pie, The Baking Collection** (1992 —  )
  Cornelius • Muffy
**Picnic** (1992-1995)
  Cornelius • Alice • Fluffy • Fuzzy • Muffy
**Yankee Doodle** (1992-1994)
  Muffy Yankee Doodle • Hoppy Uncle Sam
**Rainy Day** (1992 —  )
  Muffy • Hoppy
**The Alpine Collection, Eine Kleine Mountain Climbin;** (1992-1993, Muffy, Hoppy, Oatsie in 1994)
  Cornelius • Alice • Fluffy • Fuzzy • Muffy • Hoppy • Oatsie
**Muffy GingerBear** (1992-1992)

# A QUICK GUIDE TO MUFFY AND HER FAMILY

## 1993

**Kyoto Blossoms** (1993-1996)
Muffy • Hoppy
**Flower Festival**
Muffy • Hoppy • Oatsie (1993-1995, except for Bud & Rose) •
Lucy the Goose • Mary the Lamb • Pattie the Cow •
Rudy the Pig • Webster the Duck • Bud • Rose
**VdBeekeeping Collection, A Taste O' Honey** (1993-1996,
Muffy, Hoppy in 1997)
Cornelius • Alice • Fluffy • Fuzzy • Muffy Bumble Bee •
Hoppy Ladybug
**The Sewing Lesson** (1993 —  )
Fluffy • Muffy • Hoppy
**The Equestrienne Collection, Horsin' Around** (1993-1996)
Muffy • Hoppy • Oatsie
**The Grand Tour Collection, Travels with Muffy** (1993 —  )
Muffy
**Highland Fling, The Scottish Dance Collection** (1993-1994,
Muffy, Hoppy in 1995)
Cornelius • Alice • Fluffy • Fuzzy • Muffy • Hoppy
(Introduced with Highland Fling)
**Lulu** (1993 —  )
**Muffy Snowflake** (1993-1993)
**Muffy Rose** (1993-1995) *(Second Club Edition)*

## 1994

**Egg Painting, Walking in Eggshells** (1994-1994)
Muffy • Hoppy
**The Queen of Hearts and the Bunny Knave** (1994 —  )
Muffy • Hoppy
**The Boudoir Collection, Beauty Is Only Fur Deep** (1994 —  )
Muffy
**Tricky Treat Trio** (1994-1997)
Countess Muffula • Hoppy Harecrow • Oatsie Oaterpillar
**Bathtime Collection, Splish Splash** (1994 —  , Hoppy retired
in 1997)
Muffy • Hoppy
**Muffy of the North** (1994-1994)
**North Pole Collection, Santa's Workshop** (1994-1995, Muffy,
Hoppy, Oatsie in 1996)
Cornelius • Alice • Fluffy • Fuzzy • Muffy Santa • Hoppy Elf •
Lulu Reindeer
**Muffy 10th Anniversary** (1994-1994)
**Club House Collection** (1994 —  )
Fuzzy • Muffy • Hoppy

## 1995

**Pajama Game** (1995, Fuzzy, Fluffy in 1997)
Fluffy • Fuzzy • Muffy • Hoppy
**The Mozart Collection, One Minuet More** (1995 —  )
Muffy Mozart • Hoppy Diva

**Princess Muffy and the Pea** (1995 —  ) *(Third Club Edition)*
**All Paws on Deck** (1995 —  )
Cornelius • Alice • Fluffy • Fuzzy • Muffy • Hoppy • Lulu
**Checkmates** (1995 —  )
Muffy • Hoppy
**Czarina Muffina** (1995-1997)
**Sleddin' and Skidaddlin', A Winter Frolic** (1995 —  )
Muffy • Hoppy • Lulu
**Muffy Mouse** (1995-1995)
**New England Country Christmas** (1995-1997, except
Muffy, Hoppy)
Cornelius • Alice • Fluffy • Fuzzy • Muffy • Hoppy • Lulu

## 1996

**Paint the Town Red\*** (1996) *Limited edition to 4,500 pieces each
Cornelius • Alice
**Muffy Hearts and Flowers** (1996 —  )
**Hoppy Cocoa Bunny** (1996 —  )
**Spring Bonnets: The Silly Milly-nery Collection** (1996-1997)
Muffy • Hoppy • Lulu
**The Reading Collection, A to Z by M.V. deB** (1996 —  )
Muffy • Purrlie
**Take a Hike, A Walk on the Wylde Side** (1996 —  )
Cornelius • Alice • Fluffy • Fuzzy • Muffy • Hoppy
**Muffy Pierrot, First Collector's Edition** (1996-1996)
**Happy Birthday to You!** (1996 —  )
Muffy • Hoppy • Lulu • Oatsie
**Cheerleading: Go...Go...Go Fur It!** (1996 —  )
Muffy • Hoppy • Lulu
**Muffy the Red-Nosed ReinBear** (1996-1996)
**A Christmas Carol, Bearly in Tune** (1996- 1996, except
Muffy, Hoppy, Lulu, Oatsie)
Cornelius • Alice • Fluffy • Fuzzy • Muffy • Hoppy •
Lulu • Oatsie

## 1997

**Hoppy Messenger of Love!** (1997 —  )
**A Salad Ballad, Waltz of the Vegetables** (1997 —  )
Fluffy • Muffy • Hoppy • Lulu • Purrlie
**Square Dancing, Skip to My Lulu** (1997 —  )
Muffy • Hoppy • Lulu • Patti the Cow
**Mercy Me Hospital** (1997 —  )
Muffy • Hoppy • Lulu
**Abra-CadaBeara: "Hoppus Poke-Us"** (1997 —  )
Muffy • Hoppy
**Puttering Around** (1997 —  )
Cornelius • Alice
**Lemonade Stand** (1997 —  )
Muffy • Hoppy • Purrlie

# VanderBear Family® History

**Classic Velvet
Family**, 1983
*Left to right:* Fuzzy,
Alice, Cornelius,
Fluffy.

# The Classic Velvet Collection

Introduced in North American's 1983 catalog as "The Classic Teddy Bear Family (Jointed)".
Most were tush tag bears, available both dressed and undressed.
**20" Cornelius:** black velvet trousers, suspenders, white shirt, bow tie
**18" Alice:** black velvet drop-waist dress with lace cuffs, lace neck inset, white ribbon sash
**12" Fluffy:** black velvet smock dress with white lace collar, white headbow
**12" Fuzzy:** black velvet knickers with two buttons, white shirt, black ribbon bow tie

✳*Variation:* Alice's first dress had pearl buttons in back, the second version had snaps.

# Muffy Christening

First appeared in North American's 1994 Supplement Catalog as "The New Arrival". At 7" tall in white christening gown and cap with ribbon ties, this first Muffy was a tush tag bear and was also available without clothing.

❋*Variations (from left to right):*
**Christening I:** gown sewn shut on tush tag bear (a few issued with sewn gowns on tiny loop bear), retired
**Christening II:** gown with 2 snaps in back, some tush tag bears and some tiny loop bears, retired
**Christening III:** gown fastened with 1 button and 1 snap in back, retired
**Christening IV:** gown fastened with pink ribbon ties in back, still current
The fabric, eyelet trim, flowers, and ribbons also vary, but the different fastenings on the back of the gown are the easiest way to tell which version you have.

*Hangtag Note*
*The Christening hangtag is the same hangtag that is used on the bare Muffy. The first was a large single hangtag. Later, a small folded hangtag was used.*
*For the first few years most hangtags came with white string. After that, gold elastic cord was the most common.*

# The Red Flannel Collection

VanderBear Family Holiday Limited Edition, limited to one year of production, tush tag bears dressed for a cozy Christmas Eve supper.

**Cornelius:** red flannel robe with a black cord tie, red flannel pajama bottoms, green paisley ascot

**Alice:** red flannel nightgown, round yoke with flannel ruffle, trimmed in green at the neck

**Fluffy:** red flannel nightgown, square yoke, trimmed in green

**Fuzzy:** red flannel snap-front one piece pajamas with elastic in the back, trimmed in green

**Muffy:** red flannel gown with a square yoke, green trim at the neck, one snap in the back, red bow** on her head

**Muffy and Me™©:** red flannel gown and scarf for little girls

*\*\*Bow is attached on factory dressed bear.*

*❋Variations:*
Alice's nightgown came in two different plaids.

A few Muffys were factory dressed on the Tiny Loop bear instead of the Tush Tag bears.

Cornelius' ascot came with different background colors.

*Hangtag Note
Large white with "Muffy
VanderBear" in red and
"Holiday Collection" in green.*

# Muffy Valentine I

- White cotton eyelet dress with red ribbon sash, fastened with Velcro
- Red heart necklace
- Red headbow**

*\*\*Bow is attached on factory dressed bear.*

*Hangtag Note*
*Same size and design as Christening I*

# Cruisewear Collection
## *VanderBear Family Making Waves!*

Early bears from this group were tush tag bears.

**Cornelius:** navy flannel double breasted blazer, red and white striped jersey, white trousers, classic captain's hat

**Alice:** white pleated middy dress in a cotton blend fabric, matching beret

**Fluffy:** navy and white sailor dress with matching beret

**Fuzzy:** navy and white sailor suit with matching beret

**Muffy:** navy sailor dress with a red & white stripe insert at the neck, white trim on collar, cuffs and hem, matching beret with white trim and red pompon

**Muffy and Me™©:** sailor pinafore for girls from ages 2 to 8, with matching beret

*\*Family retired in 1988, Muffy in 1991.*

❋*Variations:* Muffy's first dress was fastened with snaps, the second with Velcro. Some variations of Cornelius came with a red hanky in his blazer pocket.

**Muffy Trivia**
Cornelius' boat was called the Merry Alice.

*Hangtag Note*
*Blue print on a white tag. The first hangtag was large, the second was standard Muffy size.*

# Muffy Halloween I: Witch

- Orange dress with pattern of black stars and white dots, black satin at the hem, yolk and cuffs of coordinated black fabric with orange stars and white dots, fastened with one large snap in the back
- Black satin cape with tied collar
- Black velveteen witch's hat trimmed in satin
- Orange pumpkin fastened to cuff
- Black felt mask with elastic strap

*Hangtag Note*
*Large 2" x 3" bright orange tag with "Muffy VanderBear" printed in black.*

# Taffeta: The Holiday Collection

VanderBear Family Holiday Limited Edition, limited to one year of production.

**Cornelius:** blue velveteen tuxedo with plaid lapels, white shirt; red bow tie, red cummerbund, and red boutonniere

**Alice:** elegant blue, green, and red plaid taffeta ball gown with puff sleeves; white eyelet ruffles on collar, cuffs, and hem; wide blue sash; separate eyelet trimmed petticoat; frilly net headpiece

**Fluffy:** a miniature version of Alice, except for a ribbon and rosette on her head

**Fuzzy:** a miniature version of Cornelius

**Muffy:** the same blue, green, red plaid taffeta ball gown as Alice and Fluffy with snap back, eyelet trim, blue grosgrain ribbon sash; blue grosgrain bow with tiny red ribbon rose** on her head; one red ribbon rose with green ribbon trim on her skirt; separate eyelet trimmed petticoat with flower pot design at the hem*

*The same eyelet fabric was used for the first version of Muffy's **Day In The Country** apron.
**Bow is attached on factory dressed bear.

Alice, Fuzzy, Fluffy, & Muffy

# A Day In The Country Collection

VanderBear Family

**Cornelius:** a country gentleman in denim overalls with plaid cuffs, sky-blue workshirt, plaid kerchief, straw hat

**Alice:** blue and white plaid dropwaisted dress, trimmed with a black bow and flowers, matching straw hat

**Fluffy:** denim pinafore, with eyelet trim and plaid pocket handkerchief, over a sky-blue eyelet trimmed blouse, straw hat trimmed with flowers

**Fuzzy:** denim overalls with blue and white plaid cuffs, a sky-blue workshirt, straw hat

**Muffy:** sky-blue smock dress, white eyelet apron, and straw hat trimmed with flowers and black band

**Muffy and Me**™©**:** Mother and daughter matching sky-blue cotton smock dresses

*\*Family retired in 1989, Muffy in 1991.*

Shown on the left is the first **Day In The Country** Muffy with "flower pot" design apron. Shown on right is the second **Day In The Country** Muffy. Behind both Muffys is the **Day In The Country Poster**, with the whole family pictured. Poster is described on page 22.

✳*Variations:*

First issue of Muffy's apron had a flower pot design at the hem (the same fabric as her Taffeta petticoat), second issue did not.

Flowers on the hat vary.

> *Hangtag Note*
> *Some of the earliest versions of the Muffy with "flower pot" apron came with a large hangtag; later versions had a small hangtag.*

# The Nutcracker Suite Collection

VanderBear Family Holiday Limited Edition, limited to one year of production.

**Cornelius:** *The Majestic Toy Soldier* in royal blue and red with gold and blue ribbon trim crossing his chest, black hat with gold trim and blue plume, black ballet shoes

**Alice:** *The Enchanting Snowflake Queen* in pale blue satin and net, trimmed in silver with a silver crown, ballet shoes

**Fluffy:** *Young Clara at the Party*, in pink taffeta trimmed in black, pantaloons, white lace head piece with pink bow, black ballet shoes

**Fuzzy:** *The Handsome Prince* in light blue velveteen suit with knickers trimmed in black ribbon, eyelet cuffs, black ribbon tie, black ballet shoes

**Muffy:** *The Magical Sugar Plum Fairy* with 4 layers of plum and blue in her net skirt sprinkled with silver, plum satin leotard with snap and flowered neckline, silver crown**, plum ballet shoes**....her first pair of shoes!

*\*\*Crown and shoes are attached on factory dressed bear.*

*Hangtag Note
First folded hangtag. White cover with blue border and nutcracker on the left. "Muffy VanderBear" and "Nutcracker Suite Collection" are printed in black. Inside you are welcomed to the performance with a brief history of the ballet and cast of characters. Yellow string was used instead of white.*

# VanderBear Hanger

Padded plush clothes hanger with bear head center

# Out of it in Africa: The Safari Collection

VanderBear Family dressed in khaki with leopard print accents for an African adventure

**Cornelius:** safari hat and binoculars

**Alice:** net covered hat and compass on belt

**Fluffy:** safari hat and black panther on leash

**Fuzzy:** safari hat and canteen

**Muffy:** khaki jumper, leopard print scarf, hat with net, camera strapped to her wrist

**Out Of It In Africa Chairs:**\*\* 20" rocker and 16" chair in natural wood with woven rattan seats

*\*Family retired in 1991, Muffy in 1992.*
*\*\*Although the Chair and Rocker were not listed in the catalog as part of the Collection, they were pictured
in the same catalog in a Safari setting containing a VanderBear hat and binoculars. Therefore, most
collectors consider them accessories to the Collection.*

✳*Variations:*
First Muffy had snaps, second had Velcro.
Alice's compass came in two sizes.

*Hangtag Note*
*Leopard print border and lion with the first gold elastic
cord. "Muffy VanderBear" and "Out of it in Africa"
are printed in black.*

# Muffy Halloween II: Black Cat
2-piece black velour catsuit with orange stitching, mask

✳*Variations:*
**First Issue:** snap back, heavy glitter on mask
**Second Issue:** tie back, less glitter on mask
**Third Issue:** tie back, silver thread stitching on mask instead of glitter

*Hangtag Note*
*Glitter Cats: First issued with large, pale orange hangtag with white string.*
*Later came with small, pale orange hangtag and white string.*
*Silver Stitched Cats: small, bright orange hangtag on gold elastic cord.*
*On all tags "Muffy VanderBear" was printed in black.*

# Furrier & Ives: The Skating Collection

VanderBear Family Holiday Limited Edition, an old-fashioned skating party, limited to one year of production.

**Cornelius:** Nordic sweater, red corduroy overalls with suspenders, black Cossack cap, black skates

**Alice:** "fur" trimmed red corduroy coat, plumed black hat, black muff, black skates

**Fluffy:** "fur" trimmed red corduroy coat with capelet, red beret, black muff, black skates

**Fuzzy:** black and green Nordic sweater, red corduroy overalls with suspenders, black Cossack hat, black skates

**Muffy:** red corduroy coat with gold buttons, white "fur" trimmed hat**, white "fur" muff with plaid ribbon around the muff and a red ribbon to go around her neck, white skates with plaid laces**

*\*\*Hats and skates are attached on factory dressed bear.*

---

*Hangtag Note*
*Black hangtag with silver border. "Muffy VanderBear," "Furrier & Ives," and "The Skating Party" are printed in white. Black*

**Muffy Trivia**
Instructions were sent to dealers for restoring bent skate blades to their original condition by covering the blade with a damp towel and lightly pressing with a hot iron.

# Muffy Valentine II

**1989-1991**

- Pink cotton dress with a double layered skirt in a tiny red heart print, heart-shaped buttons in back, collar trimmed in red satin, red ribbon sash, attached red net underskirt
- Red and pink double bow with pink rosette headbow**

*\*\*Bow is attached on factory dressed bear.*

> *Hangtag Note*
> *The hangtag for Valentine II, Valentine III, and the Bunny are all the same, with only the words "Muffy VanderBear" — see page 29. Some were hung from the top and others from the end; the colors of the printing vary from pale lavender to pink.*

**1989-1991**

# Posters, *VanderBear Family*

**Day In The Country, Out of It In Africa, Nutcracker Suite, Furrier and Ives,** and later issue **High Tea**, 18" x 24", shrink-wrapped on cardboard

**1989-retired**

# Muffy VanderBear Display

24-1/2" high x 8" deep, enclosed acrylic display case for 4 Muffys with a special section for hangtags, free-standing or wall-mounted

# Muffy Bunny

- Muffy masquerades as a VanderBunny with her own Easter basket and a pink, 2-piece, velour bunny suit.

**Muffy Trivia**
The Easter egg hunt took place on the Great Lawn of VanderBear Manor.

*Hangtag Note*
*Muffy Bunny's hangtag is the same as the one for Valentine III, see page 29.*

❋*Variations:* Muffy's first Easter basket was wicker, the second was plastic. Some of the first Bunnies <u>might</u> have come with a snap back, but most were tied.

---

# Boutique Header, *VanderBear Family*

**1989-**
<u>retired</u>

Laminated cardboard sign with easel or hanger back for display.
Spotlights VanderBears and VanderBear Wear, 12" x 16"

# The High Tea Collection

VanderBear Family dressed for High Tea in the gardens of VanderBear Manor

**Cornelius:** pink trousers, paisley suspenders, stripe shirt with white collar and cuffs, black tie

**Alice:** pink floral print pleated tea dress with white organdy collar and pleated insert and cuffs, pearls, straw hat with black trim and rose

**Fluffy:** drop waist dress in same fabric as Alice, white organdy collar, pink bow on head

**Fuzzy:** pink knickers, sailor style stripe shirt

**Muffy:** blue and white gingham check pinafore with rose pattern, white organdy blouse with appliquéd flowers on collar, bloomers, straw hat\*\* with black trim and pink bow

**White Wicker Chairs:** 7" for Muffy and 11" for Fluffy

**High Tea Note Cards:** gift package of 5 with envelopes, tied with bow

*\*Family retired in 1991, Muffy in 1992.*
*\*\*Hat is attached on factory dressed bear.*

*Hangtag Note*
*Folded hangtag that "Requests the pleasure of your company at High Tea this afternoon in the gardens of VanderBear Manor".*

❋*Variation:* A few of the first Muffy **High Teas** had a snap on the pinafore and a button on the blouse; later, both the pinafore and the blouse were fastened with Velcro.

# Muffy Pilgrim

- Black pilgrim dress with eyelet hem, white cuffs and collar, belt with buckle
- White pilgrim bonnet with ribbon tie
- Felt turkey with ribbon leash

＊*Variations:*

Some early versions came without belt and buckle, shown on left, but were made available to anyone who contacted North American Bear Company.

First belt buckles were different types of silver leatherette; later ones are silver plastic, shown on right.

Eyelet trim also varies.

# Trunk

Red plaid trunk with Muffy decal on the front, included clothing bar, two small hangers, and accessory drawer, 10" x 6" x 5".

*Variations:*

*First Trunk:* starburst design on its interior (not shown)

*Second trunk:* plain interior with red metal edging on two sides of top and bottom; sold separately or with a bare Muffy, Tree Trim outfit, and a Furrier and Ives outfit; shown on left (Original outfits packaged in trunks came without hangers and headers.)

*Third trunk:* interior printed with Muffy's signature, slightly smaller than the previous trunks, different plaid in a lighter shade with red metal edging on all four sides of top and bottom and a newly designed handle; sold separately or with a bare Muffy, Sweet Dreams outfit, and a Back to School outfit; shown on right (Original outfits packaged in trunks came without hangers and headers.).

*Rare:* solid red trunk with decal and starburst interior issued for a short time before first plaid version was available.

# The Tree Trimming Collection

VanderBear Family Holiday Limited Edition, Christmas at home, limited to one year of production

**Cornelius:** black watch-plaid jacket and twill pants, candy stripe dickey, holiday bow tie, monogrammed velvet slippers

**Alice:** lace-trimmed robe, Christmas tree earrings, corduroy slippers

**Fluffy:** black watch-plaid dress with candy cane trim, organdy apron, matching headbow, Mary Jane shoes

**Fuzzy:** plaid rompers and Christmas bow tie

**Muffy:** white organdy pinafore with red trim and candy cane appliqué on collar, red and white candy-striped cotton smock dress, green and red plaid head bow**, gingerbread cookie charm sewn into her pocket (**first charm of her collection**), and her first pair of Mary Jane shoes - red

**Scottie VanderDog:** 4" black plush puppy in a red cardboard kennel with a green plaid bow, FD only

**Muffy's Christmas Tree I:** 9" tree with gingerbread ornaments, glass balls, tiny presents, white ribbon, baby's breath, red garland, and apples - according to NABCO only 15,000 were made *(See Variations on next page.)*

# The Tree Trimming Collection

**1989-**
**1989**

**Muffy's Cookie Plate:** 3 little gingerbread cookies arranged on a red and green holly plate, packaged in cellophane with header

**VanderBear Family Sofa:** green moiré camel-back sofa, 34"W x 19"H x 19"D

*\*\*Bow is attached on factory dressed bear.*

*\*Variations:*

Shown below: two of ***many*** variations of the Tree Trimming Christmas Tree

The Tree on the left has 4 gingerbread ornaments that are fastened to the tree by a loop on their heads. The base is the same on all four sides.

The Tree on the right has 6 gingerbread ornaments, but only 1 is fastened to the tree with a loop on its head, the other 5 are glued onto the tree. The base has a different Santa picture on each side.

*Hangtag Note*
*Folded hangtag opens to reveal a Holiday letter from the VanderBears. Their new settee for the drawing room is mentioned as well as Muffy's new puppy.*

## Muffy Trivia
Scottie VanderDog was pictured in the 1989 catalog with a solid green bow, but it was plaid when he arrived. The Spring 1990 catalog pictures Scottie with a leash, but it was never produced...perhaps that is why he ran away in the summer of 1990.

# Muffy Angel

- Holiday Boxed Limited Edition
- Heavenly Blue gown sprinkled with stars and trimmed with gold, separate gold petticoat
- Embossed foil wings and halo with stars
- Hand-tied into an ornate Renaissance-style box with Certificate of Authenticity on inside cover
- Factory Dressed only

**Muffy Trivia**
Muffy wore her Italian Renaissance Angel costume for her kindergarten Holiday Play. Even though the catalog showed Muffy's halo without stars, they all came with stars.

*Hangtag Note*
*The bottom line reads,*
*"Limited Holiday Edition 1989."*

# Greeting/Christmas Cards

Boxed sets with 20 cards and 21 envelopes, *Furrier & Ives, Tree Trimming, Muffy Angel*

1989 Greeting Cards; 1992 Pop-up cards; 1992 Holiday Stickers, Gift Tags, and Sticker Book. See descriptions on page 55 & 63.

# Muffy Valentine III

- Heart-strewn romper with pink rick-rack trim, tied in back
- Pink Mary Janes
- Pink headbow**
- Valentine card tied to her wrist

**Bow is attached on factory dressed bear.*

*Variations:
Background colors vary between cream, on right, and white, on left.
Early versions came with darker pink shoes.

1990
**MUFFY & FUZZY** issued undressed for Valentine's Day with red Valentine ribbons and tags

> *Hangtag Note*
> *The same hangtag was used for Valentine II and Bunny*

# Muffy St. Patrick's Day

**1990**

White cotton dress with green shamrock print, eyelet trimmed hem, green check cuffs and collar, green check bloomers, green check headbow**, green Mary Janes

**Bow is attached on factory dressed bear.*

*Variations:
Check trim on earlier Muffys was larger and yellowish green, shown on left; the newer version is smaller and bright green, shown on right.
Eyelet trim also varies.

> *Hangtag Note*
> *Special hangtag gives Muffy the Irish name of "Muffeen."*

> **Muffy Trivia**
> Muffy's dress was sent to her by friends in Ireland to wear in the St. Patrick's Day Parade.

# Muffy Chick

Easter playsuit in yellow velour with chick head cap and wings tied with orange ribbon, orange Mary Janes

*Variations:*

Old and new versions came with gold beaks; the middle came with a yellow beak.

First issued without black stitching all the way around the eyes, shown on left.

---

# Muffy Beach

**1990**

**Muffy:** red print cotton bikini, matching kerchief, white monogrammed terry cloth towel (outfit packaged with Muffy cutout)

**Deck Chair and Umbrella:** red and white stripe chair with monogrammed umbrella, outfit packaged with header

*Variations:*

First issued with snap on back of bikini top; later issued with all elastic.

The first and latest versions of the deck chair fabric have narrow woven stripes that are the same color of red on both the top and underneath. A version in the middle had wider and brighter red stripes on a more open weave fabric that was printed on the top side only.

**Muffy Trivia**
Muffy wore her new bathing suit on the beach in France during the family's trip to Gibearny.

# Gibearny: An Impressionist Collection

VanderBear Family, inspired by their visit to the French gardens of Gibearny made famous by Monet's impressionistic Water Lily paintings

**Cornelius:** artist's smock, dickey, cravat, hanky, corduroy pants, straw hat, pince-nez glasses

**Alice:** flowered voile dress with organdy collar, water lily headpiece

**Fluffy:** floral print dress with organdy collar, Mary Janes, water lily headpiece

**Fuzzy:** 2 piece linen sailor suit, rubber frog

**Muffy:** floral smock, lavender pinafore, lavender Mary Janes, water lily headpiece**, paint tube charm (with "Muffy" on it) sewn into her pocket (*second charm in her collection*), palette on her paw

**Garden Bench:** rustic wooden French bench with rattan covered arms and seat, 21" x 17" x 9"

*\*\*Headpiece is attached on factory dressed bear.*

❋*Variation:*
Cornelius' first hat was more flat with rolled brim. Later hats were rounded without rolled brim.
Earlier Muffys <u>might</u> have had a button, but most were fastened with Velcro.

# Back To School

**Muffy:** black and white number-print dress with white trim, red beret, red Mary Janes, school bag

**Hoppy, Muffy's new friend is introduced:** red and white number-print dress with white trim, black beret, black Mary Janes, school bag

**Watches:** black and red watch with Muffy's picture, red or black strap, gift box

**School Desk:** red wooden desk with Muffy's signature on the front, 7" x 5" x 6"

**Notebook:** old-fashioned red and black notebook with Muffy illustration on the front, black ribbon ties, 5" x 6-3/4"

*Muffy's Desk retired in 1992, the remainder of the collection retired in 1993.*

**Muffy Trivia**

Hoppy became Muffy's "bosom bunny". Hoppy's parents travel a lot (which is not unusual for a family of rabbits). When they are gone, Hoppy stays with the VanderBears and joins them in many of their adventures.

# Remembearances:
# A Wedding Collection

A romantic glance backwards...

**Cornelius:** black tails, pique dickey and vest, cravat, top hat

**Alice:** white moiré taffeta, lace and tulle bridal ensemble; garter; bouquet

*Hangtag Note
Oval insert on gold
tag printed with
"Remembearances"
and either Alice or
Cornelius' name.*

# Stationery, *VanderBear*

Each gift packaged with 5 cards and 5 envelopes: ***Day in the Country, Gibearny,
Remembearance, High Tea*** (***High Tea Stationery*** was first issued as note cards
with the ***High Tea Collection*** in 1989.)

# Sweet Dreams:
# The Victorian Sleepwear Collection

VanderBear Family dressed in old-fashioned nightwear

**Cornelius:** monogrammed nightshirt and cap

**Alice:** peignoir and sleepcap

**Fluffy:** lace-tucked gown and cap

**Fuzzy:** monogrammed shirt and nightcap

**Muffy:** pajamas and bed jacket tied with satin ribbon, satin ribbon around her head**

**Muffy's Teddy Bear:** 3" brown felt bear with red plaid bow in red shopping bag, packaged in cellophane with header

*The family and Muffy's Teddy Bear retired in 1992, Muffy in 1993.*
**Ribbon is attached on factory dressed bears.*

✴*Variations:*

First issue was in thin cotton.

Second issue was a cotton blend with less wrinkles.

Lace also varies.

*Hangtag Note*
*White tag with very thin gold cord. Both "Muffy VanderBear" and "Sweet Dreams" are printed in pale blue.*

**Muffy Trivia**
Alice makes secret milk (warm milk and honey) for Fluffy, Fuzzy, and Muffy at bedtime.

# Musical Soireé:
# The Purple Velvet Collection

VanderBear Family Holiday Limited Edition, celebrating a musical Victorian Christmas
   at home

**Cornelius:** white tie, breeches and tails, damask waistcoat, lace cuffs

**Alice:** décolleté evening gown with lavender bows, purple choker, feathered headdress,
   bouquet of flowers

**Fluffy:** velvet dress, white lace trimmed collar, lavender sash with rose, lavender headbow

**Fuzzy:** Little Lord "Fauntlebear" velvet suit

**Muffy:** velvet smock dress with white pique collar and cuffs, lavender ribbon rose,
   ribboned pantaloons, purple Mary Janes, plaid headbow**

**Musical Soireé Christmas Tree II:** 18" Victorian fir; trumpet, French horn, and violin
   ornaments; musical stave paper base; purple ribbons and bows; baby's breath;
   plastic display box

**Chaise Lounge:** purple moiré settee, black tassels and trim, no back, 16" x 35" x 16"

**Muffy's Stradibearius:** 5" wooden violin in purple illustrated box with cellophane
   window. "Muffy VanderBear" and "Stradebearius" are printed on the box

*Family retired in 1991, Stradibearius, Chaise Lounge, and Tree in 1990, Muffy in 1992.*
**Bow is attached on factory dressed bears.*

✳*Variations:*

The tag on the inside of Muffy's first dress is printed "Vintage Collection," later changed to
   "Musical Soiree."

The fabric and lace on Muffy's dress vary.

> **Muffy Trivia**
> Muffy took violin
> lessons from
> Madam
> Bearloska.

> *Hangtag Note*
> *Ivory tag with pur-*
> *ple border and*
> *music motif. "Muffy*
> *VanderBear" and*
> *"Musical Soireé"*
> *are printed in*
> *purple.*

**1990-1990**

# Muffy Little Fir Tree

- Holiday Boxed Limited Edition
- Organdy and satin, red and green tree-inspired dress
- Star and holly headdress, attached
- Green satin slippers
- "Partridge in a Bear Tree" on right paw
- Victorian style gift box with certificate of authenticity on the back
- Factory Dressed only

**Muffy Trivia**
Muffy's Fir Tree costume was for the Teddy Bear Fancy Dress Ball.

---

**1990**

# Armoire

- Country-style wood with top shelf and 2 bottom drawers, 16-1/2" x 13-1/2" x 7-3/4"

*Variations:*
Both the Armoire and Sleigh Bed were issued in a variety of different wood shades, according to availability. Early issues were much lighter.

The plaque or decal on the foot of the bed and on the front of the Armoire also varies.

*Shown :* Muffy's Bed and Armoire Bedding Accessories (introduced in 1991) First Armoire Accessories (introduced in 1991)

---

**1990**

# Sleigh Bed

Wood with monogram at the foot: comes with white mattress and lace-trimmed pillow with embroidered monogram, 6" x 14-1/2" x 7-1/2"

---

**1990-1995**

# Muffy VanderBear Club Membership Kit

Members receive a ribbon-tied portfolio containing Membership Card and Certificate, **Back to School** Stationery, Muffy Logo Pendant, 10 Stickers, and a Photo Album of Muffy's Collections. Also included is a subscription to Muffy's own newsletter, *Fanfare*, published 3 times a year. New Muffy VanderBear Club Kit available in 1996, contains linen covered Collection Album. Original Kit pictured on page 97.

# Mommy and Me:
# The Teacup Collection

Mother and daughter tea party

**Alice:** blue print teacup and pansy print dress with shawl collar, organza headbow, nosegay of flowers on her wrist

**Muffy:** the same print dress with yellow accents, organza headbow**, yellow Mary Janes, a card for mother tied to her wrist that says "I Love You, xxoo, Muffy"

**Frame:** ribbon and pansy motif on resin frame with a picture of Muffy, 2-3/4" x 3-1/4", boxed in white VdB logo box with plastic cover

**Tea Set:** personalized Muffy-size tea set with pansy motif, 12 pieces, box is illustrated with picture of collection

**Teatime Settee:** wicker garden settee, blue tea cup print cushion with pink piping, 17" x 11"

**Teatime Table:** wicker with blue accent, 5" x 7" in diameter

**Teatime Chair:** wicker, blue accent, blue teacup print cushion with pink piping, 7"

*\*\*Bow is attached on factory dressed bear.*

*Hangtag Note*
*White tag with triple border and pansy at the top. "Muffy VanderBear" and "The Teacup Collection" are printed in blue.*

**Muffy Trivia**
For Mother's Day, Muffy plans a tea party and serves Alice tea in the garden. Muffy's gift to Alice was a framed photo of herself.
Pictured in the catalog are plain fabric cushions with teacup piping on the chair and settee. According to NABCO only a few of these were made.

# Easter Fantasy

**Muffy:** pink organdy pinafore with embroidered butterfly and flower basket on her pocket, bloomers, hemp Easter bonnet** with flowers, basket with chick tied to her wrist

**Hoppy:** yellow organdy pinafore with embroidered carrot pocket, bloomers, bonnet with carrots, basket with bunny on her wrist

*\*\*Hat is attached on factory dressed bear.*

✵*Variations:* Last issue of Muffy wore a lighter pink pinafore and her hat had a hemp hat band.

*Hangtag Note*
*White background with pale pink and green borders.*
*"Muffy VanderBear" and "Easter Fantasy" are printed*
*in pale pink.*

# The Wild West:
# A Traveling Rodeo Show

1991-
1994

VanderBear Family goes West!

**Cornelius,** *Paw***:** fringed jacket, jeans, bandanna, cowboy hat

**Alice,** *Ma***:** chambray poke bonnet, bandanna print dress

**Fluffy,** *Pawcahontas***:** Indian princess in fringed dress and feathered headdress

**Fuzzy,** *The Kid***:** chaps, western shirt, bandanna, cowboy hat

**Muffy,** *Miss Muffy***:** red gingham dress, bandanna print smock with blue chambray hankie sewn in front pocket, cowboy hat, red Mary Janes

**Oatsie:** 9" spotted Appaloosa one-trick pony, Muffy's newest friend, issued factory dressed only in western gear, western outfit was never issued separately.

*Folded hangtag is an advertisement for "The VanderBear Traveling Wild West Show"*
*and gives "Miss Muffy" the title of "The Littlest Cowpoke." Inside you are invited to*
*"step right up" and Oatsie "the wonder pony" is introduced.*

**Muffy Trivia**
"Hopp-a-long" Hoppy could not go to the *Wild West* because she had Rocky Mountain Spring Fever. Even though the catalog pictured Muffy in boots, she only wore red Mary Janes.

## 1991

# Paw de Deux
### *Ballerinas at ballet class*

**Muffy:** tutu, pink leotard, pink ballet shoes**, flowered headband**
**Hoppy:** tutu, blue leotard, blue ballet shoes, headbow

*\*\*Headband and shoes are attached on factory dressed bear.*

*Hangtag Note White background with pink and blue border. "Muffy VanderBear" and "Paw de Deux" are printed in pink.*

✳*Variation:* Later outfits packaged on Muffy and Hoppy cutouts, color varies.

## 1991- 1992

# Armoire Accessories

Muffy's signature blue fabric-covered closet set: hatbox, shoe chest (for 4 pairs), and four fabric hangers, boxed. *Accessories pictured on page 36.*

# Underthings

- Muffy and Hoppy
- Each set includes teddy, bloomers, and panties; packaged as outfits only on Muffy and Hoppy cutouts, with headers and hangers.
- No hangtag included.

# Bedding Accessories

Muffy's signature blue fabric bed set: pillow, pillow case, sheet, and quilt, packaged with header and Muffy cutout. *Accessories pictured on page 36.*

# The Fortune Tellers

Magical costumes for Halloween

**Muffy Gypsy:** peasant-style paisley dress, satin stripe apron with gold coins, matching vest and slippers\*\*, gypsy headscarf with attached golden earrings

**Hoppy Genie:** fringed midriff top, brocade bloomers with golden coins, feathered turban, slippers with curled toes

**Fortune Telling Accessories:** crystal ball, bearot cards, magic lamp, "flying" carpet, boxed

*\*\*Slippers are attached on factory dressed bear.*

# The Ballet Recital

**Muffy:** tulle and satin recital costume, sparkling toe shoes, silvery crown,
   pink flowers tied to her paw
**Hoppy:** similar to Muffy's costume with different trims and purple flowers in her paw

*✷Variation:* Later outfits
   packaged on Muffy
   and Hoppy cutouts.

*Hangtag Note*
*White background with lavender border. "Muffy*
*VanderBear" and "Ballet Recital" are in lavender.*

**Muffy Trivia**
Muffy and Hoppy's first
dance performance was
"Chopawniana."

# Muffy Postcard & Button I

**1991-1995**

With original Muffy portrait logo
*Logo and postcard are pictured on page 98.*

# Muffy SnowBear

- Holiday Boxed Limited Edition
- Fluffy white snowsuit with "coal" buttons
- Carrot nose
- Plaid scarf
- Twig Broom
- Black hat with cardinal and sprig of holly
- Illustrated box (reminiscent of a Victorian Christmas Card) with certificate of authenticity on the back
- Factory Dressed only

**Muffy Trivia**
Muffy wore her Snowbear costume to go caroling.

*Hangtag Note*
*White background with slate blue border. "Muffy VanderBear" and "SnowBear" are printed in the same blue color.*

# Bal Masqué:
# The Legendary Party Collection

VanderBear Family Holiday masqueraders at the Commedia Dell'Arte Ball in a 16th Century** Italian Comedy

**Cornelius:** "Gilles" in white satin, crimson bows on his slippers, ruffled collar, hat, mask

**Alice:** "Pierrette" in harlequin print Panier-style dress, ruffled collar, black satin slippers, feather tricorn hat, mask

**Fluffy:** "Columbine" in harlequin print dress, black satin slippers, feathered tricorn hat, mask

**Fuzzy:** "Harlequin" in ruffled collared jacket with pompons, matching pants, black satin slippers, feathered tricorn hat, mask

**Muffy:** "Infanta" in gold-trimmed pink moiré taffeta gown with peplum, floral ribbon sash with gold bow, black shoes with laces, floral feathered headbow, mask on stick

**Hoppy:** "Lapina" in gold-trimmed blue moiré taffeta gown with ruffled collar, floral ribbon sash with gold bow, black shoes with laces, floral feathered head piece, mask on stick

**Oatsie:** "Octavio" in collar and mask, *the first time Oatsie was available both dressed and undressed.* Oatsie is described on page 39.

**Bal Masque Recamier:** magenta pink moiré fainting couch, 37" x 16" x 16"

* *Family and Recaimer retired in 1992; Muffy, Hoppy, & Oatsie in 1993. Bal Masque was the first Hoppy and Oastie to retire.*
** *16th Century is used in the catalog, but the tag reads 17th Century.*

> *Hangtag Note*
> *Folded fan-shaped hangtag on wrist with tassel, inside*
> *is an invitation to the ball.*

# Muffy Butterfly

First Boxed Limited Edition of 10,000 to commemorate the formation of the Muffy VanderBear Club, for Club members only

- Blue velvet and gold net butterfly suit with gold ruffled collar, jewels, and ribbons
- Blue and green felt wings with gold painted veins
- Blue velvet slippers with a jewel on each curled and pointed toe
- Blue velvet cap with jewels, antennae, and gold tie
- Crystal wand with butterflies, ribbons, and flowers tied to right paw
- Presentation box with butterfly wing opening
- Certificate of Authenticity with LE number
- Factory Dressed only

*Also shown on Front Cover.*

> *Hangtag Note*
> *Round blue tag with "Muffy VanderBear," "Butterfly," and the border in gold.*

### Muffy Trivia
It was announced in the Winter 1990 issue of the *North American Bear News* that there would be a special LE Muffy available at a Muffy Convention planned for May 1991 in Chicago. The theme of the Convention was to have been *Muffy's Midsummer Night's Dream*. However in the following issue of the *NABCO News*, the Convention was postponed and that special LE Muffy became the first Club Piece — *Muffy Butterfly*!

# Down On The Farm

**Muffy:** blue and white checked sundress with floral borders, kerchief, blue shoes with yellow laces, sack of *Muffy's Farm Feed* tied to wrist

**Muffy's Farm Friends:** Patti The Cow, Mary The Lamb, Rudy The Pig, Lucy The Goose, Webster The Duck in gingham bows, factory dressed only

**Farm Cart:** rustic wooden cart with Muffy's signature on the back, 10-3/4" x 4-1/2" x 4-1/2"

*\*The Farm Cart was retired in the Spring of 1997, but was sold out before the end of 1996.*

※*Variations:*

The wheels on the first cart (shown on left) were hand crafted, while the second cart (shown on right), has die cut wheels.

According to the catalog and *NABCO News*, Muffy's first shoes had pale green laces.

> **Muffy Trivia**
> The farm that Muffy visits belongs to her mother's friend "Aunt Beatrice" in the "Bearkshires".

## 1992-1995

## Dutch Treat

**Muffy:** delft blue print dress, cap with golden braids, red tulip in left paw, hand-carved wooden shoes

**Hoppy:** delft blue pantaloons and smock, white flowers on bodice, cap with braids, hand-carved wooden shoes

*Hangtag Note*
*Round tag with blue and yellow border. "Muffy VanderBear" and "Dutch Treat" are printed in blue.*

## 1992

## Muffy Mail

**Gift Enclosure** with envelopes in 3 designs: Muffy Cherub, Hoppy Cherub, Hoppy and Muffy Friendship

**Greeting Cards** with envelopes in 3 designs: Muffy and Hoppy Heart, Muffy and Dove, Muffy and Oatsie

**Stationery Set**, notepaper with envelopes, package of 8 each in 2 designs: Muffy and Dove, Hoppy and Muffy Friendship

**Postcard Set**, portfolio of 9 cards, 3 each of: Muffy and Oatsie; Muffy and Hoppy Cherubs; Muffy, Hoppy and Oatsie with cart

**Sticker Book:** 24 stickers in above designs

**Counter Display Unit** for Muffy Mail is 11" x 9" x 7"

# Cherry Pie: The Baking Collection

**1992**

"Daddy and Me at Patisserie V de B"

**Cornelius:** monogrammed toque blanc (chef's hat), apron, plaid shirt, green pants, quilted oven mitt

**Muffy:** cherry print dress with plaid collar and white eyelet apron with cherry embroidered pocket, quilted potholder tied to her wrist, red shoes, green headbow**

**Pie Cupboard:** cherry motifs and Muffy's signature on white wooden pie safe with mesh windows, 11" x 6" x 3"

**Cherry Pie:** cherry pie with Muffy's signature pricked in crust, boxed in "VdeB Patisserie" bakery box, 2-3/4" diameter x 3/4" thick

***Bow is attached on factory dressed bear*

# Picnic Collection

VanderBear Family picnic outing in VanderBear Woods

**Cornelius:** chambray shorts, "goin' fishin" print shirt, checked ascot, pork-pie hat, fishing creel with hangtag, 3-1/2" x 5" x 4"

**Alice:** checked porch dress with white pique napkin print cuffs and pocket flaps, straw and fabric hat

**Fluffy:** checked sundress with white pique napkin print trim, bouquet on bodice, peek-a-boo hat

**Fuzzy:** chambray overalls, checked cuffs, "goin' fishin" shirt, 10" bamboo fishing pole with fish

**Muffy:** checked sundress with white pique collar and pocket flaps with berry print accents, straw picture bonnet with meadow flowers

**Tablecloth Set:** floral and checked "VdeB" monogrammed tablecloth, 21" x 21", and 4 matching napkins, 8" x 8", packaged with header and hangtag

**\*Picnic Set:** cardboard box printed in wicker design, 4-1/2" x 1-1/2 " x 3-1/2": 4 tiny 3-1/4" spoons, 4 printed tin 3-1/8" plates, and 13" x 13" signature tablecloth

*\* The Picnic Set, which was originally supposed to be packaged in a wicker basket, retired in 1993, but was sold out before the end of 1992. Family retired Spring 1995, Muffy retired Spring 1996.*

**Muffy Trivia**
Hoppy missed the picnic because of a terrible case of the sniffles.

*Hangtag Note*
*Folded Hangtag*

# Rainy Day

**Muffy:** bright yellow rain slicker, Sou'western hat, red and yellow boots

**Hoppy:** blue slicker with hood, blue and yellow boots

**Rainy Day Umbrella:** personalized, packaged with header

**Rainy Day Puzzle**: introduced in the 1993 Spring catalog, 221 pieces, boxed, 14" x 10" when completed

\* *Due to production problems, this collection was not available in stores until 1993.*

✳*Variation:*

The first versions of the raincoats were shiny, slick fabric. Later versions were a heavier fabric with more texture. This later version of Muffy's slicker was also a lighter yellow. Muffy's first raincoat also had an unfinished hem, but in 1996 her raincoat was stitched at the hem.

> *Hangtag Note*
> *Blue tag with "Muffy VanderBear" in yellow and "Rainy Day" in white.*

# Scarf

## *Life Is One Big Dress Up*

First renewal gift for Muffy VanderBear Club second year members, pink cotton scarf featuring Muffy in 16 outfits, 20-1/2" x 20-1/2". *Pictured on page 97.*

# Yankee Doodle

Red, white, and blue Fourth of July finery

**Muffy Yankee Doodle:** colonial frock, feathered tricorn hat**, ribbon lace-up red shoes

**Hoppy Uncle Sam:** top hat, rompers, tails, bow tie, ribbon lace-up black shoes

*\*\*Hat is attached on factory dressed bear.*

*Hangtag
Note
Round tag
with star
border.
"Muffy
VanderBear"
in blue and
"Yankee
Doodle" in
red.*

# Eine Kliene Mountain Climbin':
# The Alpine Collection

VanderBear Family Holiday in the Alps with traditional Tyrolean folk costumes.

**Cornelius:** felt vest with woven trim and painted wooden buttons, pique peasant shirt, felt lederhosen with embroidered VdeB logo, plaid tie, felt hat with feather

**Alice:** dirndl dress with plaid shawl, felt hat with feather and bird

**Fluffy:** dirndl dress with pique bodice, plaid apron, felt hat with bird

**Fuzzy:** lederhosen, painted wooden buttons, suspenders, peasant blouse, print tie, hat with feather

**Muffy:** green felt jacket, red felt skirt, Alpine floral braid, felt hat with plaid ribbon and feather

**Hoppy:** felt jacket and skirt with floral braid, felt braided hat

**Oatsie:** felt blanket, hat, ribbon reins

**Muffy's Alpine Sleigh:** wooden, edelweiss motif, personalized, 12" x 9" x 5"

**Muffy's Alpine Tree:** bird & bell ornaments, cuckoo clocks, edelweiss, woven ribbon trim, bluebird on top (signifies happiness and good fortune), 10", boxed

\* *Family retired in 1993; Muffy, Hoppy, Oatsie, and accessories in 1994.*

✳*Variation:* First sleigh came with green runners, second had red runners.

*Hangtag Note*
*Folded Hangtag. First Hoppys issued with hangtag that said "Hoppy VanderBear" instead of "VanderHare." This was later corrected.*

**Muffy Trivia**
Cornelius built the Alpine Sleigh for Muffy.

# Muffy GingerBear

- Holiday Boxed Limited Edition
- Cookie outfit in brown velour with white "icing" and "gumdrop" buttons
- Gingerbread recipe card tied to wrist
- Gingerbread house gift box with instructions and patterns for making a Muffy cookie house, with certificate of authenticity on the back
- Factory Dressed only

**Muffy Trivia**
Muffy wore her Gingerbread costume to perform at the Chalet during the family's Alpine Adventure.

# Ornaments

First 4 of a series of hand painted resin ornaments based on limited edition Muffys
**Angel, Little Fir Tree, SnowBear, GingerBear:** 2-1/2" x 3", boxed

Series of 14
ornaments
issued
between 1992
and 1994

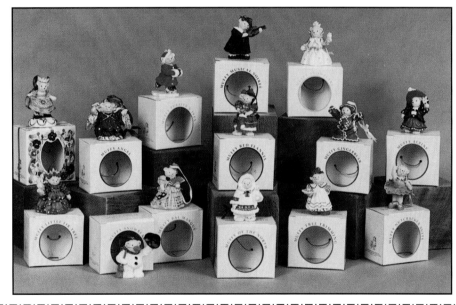

# Holiday Gift Tags & Stickers

Featuring Muffy, Hoppy, and Oatsie: 8 gift tags, 3" x 3-1/2", packaged with header and 24 stickers packaged with header. *Tags and Stickers are pictured on page 28.*

# Pop-Up Cards

Old fashioned diecut, 4" x 6-1/2" with envelope in cellophane bag, *Sweet Dreams, Furrier & Ives, Musical Soiree, Tree Trimming. Cards are pictured on page 28. Catalog lists **Bal Masque**, but this was not produced as a Pop-up card.*

# Kyoto Blossoms

**1993\***
**-1996**

In honor of the annual Japanese celebration of the Cherry Blossom Festival in Kyoto

**Muffy:** blue kimono with cherry blossom motif, obi sash, matching headbow** with flowers

**Hoppy:** cherry pink kimono with the same design as Muffy's, obi sash, matching headbow with flowers

**Kyoto Blossom Accessories:** "pokuri" (traditional Japanese sandals) washi paper fan, a fabric bag that matches their obi sashes, packaged in an authentic "tomoebako" box

*\* Although part of the 1993 Spring Collection, Kyoto blossoms was available in the stores in November of 1992.*
*\*\*Bow is attached on factory dressed bear.*

# Flower Festival

**1993-**
**1995\***

A May Day celebration in the Wildflower Garden of VanderBear Manor to introduce *Muffy's new rabbit friends, Bud and Rose*

**Muffy:** pink dotted Swiss dress with floral trim, pink bloomers, flower garland headband**

**Hoppy:** aqua dotted Swiss dress with floral trim, aqua bloomers, flower garland headbow

**Muffy's Flower Festival Friends:** Oatsie, Lucy the Goose, Mary the Lamb, Patti the Cow, Rudy the Pig, Webster the Duck, Bud, Rose, all with floral garlands

**Flower Garlands:** for Muffy's friends (accept for Bud and Rose) with instructions, packaged with header

**Muffy Trivia**
Bud and Rose are Hoppy's cousins.

*\*Bud and Rose were not retired with the rest of the Collection. Factory dressed Muffy, Muffy outfit, and Hoppy outfit were sold out before the end of 1994.*
*\*\*Garland is attached on factory dressed bear.*

# VdBeekeeping Collection
## *A Taste O' Honey*

VanderBear Family on their honey farm

**Cornelius:** black and white cotton ticking overalls with beehive pocket label and beehive bordered neckerchief

**Alice:** striped ticking pinafore with beehive pocket label and floral bordered scarf

**Fluffy:** striped ticking pinafore with bee pocket label on bodice, floral bordered neckerchief

**Fuzzy:** ticking overalls with bee pocket label, beehive bordered neckerchief

**Muffy Bumble Bee:** velvety striped romper with daisy on bodice, felt antennae and embroidered wings attached to hood, black Mary Janes

**Hoppy Ladybug:** black velvety jumpsuit, felt antennae, scalloped collar and spotted felt ladybug wing attached to hood, red Mary Janes

**Large Honey Jar:** porcelain with floral motif, Muffy Bumble Bee on lid, 6" wooden dipper with ladybug handle, 6-1/4" x 5-1/4", boxed

**Small Honey Jar:** porcelain with Muffy's name written in leaves, bee on lid, 3-3/4" wooden dipper with lady bug handle, 3-1/2" x 3", boxed

**Sticker Book:** 50 stickers that tell the story of *The VdBeeKeeping Tale*

*\*Family retired Fall 1996; Muffy, Hoppy, Honey Jars, and Sticker Book retired 1997.*

✳*Variation:*

Muffy's bee wings were made of a finer and whiter fabric in the later versions.

*Hangtag Note*
*Folded hangtag in the shape of a beehive.*

# Sewing Lesson Collection

Fluffy helps Muffy and Hoppy make aprons.

**Fluffy:** pique pinafore, stripe dress, tape measure headbow

**Muffy:** yellow smocked dress in custom printed fabric, tied in back; yellow tape measure headbow**, spring green new style T-strap shoes

**Hoppy:** lavender smock in custom fabric with front Velcro closing, lavender tape measure headbow, coral pink T-strap shoes

**Collectors Thimbles:** 3 porcelain thimbles with a portrait of each (Fluffy, Hoppy, and Muffy) in box covered with Muffy's yellow dress fabric, box: 2" x 4" x 2-1/4", thimbles: 1-1/8" x 1"

**Muffy's Sewing Tin:** double-handled tin with fabric to make 2 aprons for Muffy and Hoppy, pattern with Muffy's instructions, 4 scissors and thimble buttons on card, hangtag, 3" x 3-1/2" x 2-5/16"

*\*\*Bow is attached on factory dressed bear.*

# Horsin' Around:
# The Equestrienne Collection

**Muffy:** black English style riding jacket, eyelet dickey, white jodhpurs with "chamois" inserts, laced paddock boots, top hat with organza bow

**Hoppy:** riding coat, dickey, khaki jodhpurs with "chamois" inserts, laced paddock boots, derby hat with organza bow

**Oatsie:** jockey cap with bow, bridle, leatherette saddle with gold monogram and red ribbon tie

## *VanderBear Family in* New Fur

It more closely matches the original golden tan fur.

# Tote Bag

2nd renewal gift for Muffy Club 3rd year members: blue bordered canvas bag with colorful Muffys & fans, 14-1/2" x 10-1/2" x 3". *Bag is pictured on page 97.*

# Birthday Card I

From Muffy to Club members: accordion folded Muffy cutouts. *Card is pictured on page 98.*

# Travels with Muffy:
# The Grand Tour Collection

**Muffy:** twill coat with plaid buttons, velvet collar and cuffs, passport tied into her pocket, velvety shoes and hat with plaid ribbon

**Muffy Travel Diary:** travel notes on back, 200 pages, 6-1/4" x 6-1/4"

**Muffy Travel Watch:** Muffy on top of the world, her hat is the second hand, navy blue band in tin case

---

**1993**

# Lulu

A 5" Scottish MacFluff with plaid neckbow, FD only

**Lulu's Bed:** tartan, personalized

**Lulu's Brush:** wooden, red strap

**Lulu's Bowl:** red tin, personalized

**Lulu's Tag & Leash:** red leash and personalized dog tag

*Note:* All accessories are packaged on headers.

*Hangtag Note*
*Single tag in the Highland Fling crest shape with "Muffy's Dog Lulu" printed in yellow. This original tag was replaced on Lulu in 1996.*

**Muffy Trivia**
Muffy found Lulu on the grounds of MacVanderBearn Castle.

# A Highland Fling:
# The Scottish Collection

VanderBear Family Holiday in Scotland at MacVanderBearn Castle

**Cornelius:** gold trimmed velveteen jacket, ribbon necktie with thistle accent, thistle corduroy vest with VdeB buttons, Malcolm tartan kilt, dickey, Scottish hat, argyle socks, gillie shoes

**Alice:** cutaway jacket with insignia buttons, lace jabot with thistle, velveteen skirt, Scottish hat, gillie shoes

**Fluffy:** argyle sweater, fringed Malcolm tartan skirt, tam, argyle socks, gillie shoes

**Fuzzy:** argyle sweater, velveteen pantaloons, Scottish hat, argyle socks, gillie shoes

**Muffy:** red sweater, Malcolm tartan skirt with fringed hem and front sporran pocket with tassel, tartan sash, corduroy tam** with pompon and yellow ribbon, argyle socks, gillie shoes

**Hoppy:** yellow sweater with thistle, fringed tartan circle skirt with pocket, velveteen pantaloons, tam, gillies

**Snowdome:** among the ruins of the castle tower, boxed, 6" x 18" around

**Wreath:** 12" with Scottish ornaments, boxed

**Stocking:** quilted illustrations, 12" x 8", packaged with header

*The Family, Snowdome, Wreath, and Stocking retired in 1994, Muffy and Hoppy retired in 1995.*
**Tam is attached on factory dressed bear.*

---

*Hangtag Note*
*Folded*

---

**Muffy Trivia**
The family wears kilts in the Malcolm plaid, Cornelius' Uncle's clan.

# Muffy Snowflake

- Holiday Boxed Limited Edition
- Silvery snowflake costume with snowflake pattern cut into jacket and velvet skirt with silver snowflakes
- Sparkling net underskirt
- Snowflake crown, attached
- Iridescent wand
- Illustrated ice palace box with certificate of authenticity on the back
- Factory Dressed only

*Hangtag Note*
*Sky blue tag with snowflake motif. "Muffy VanderBear" and "Snowflake" are in purple.*

**Muffy Trivia**
Fluffy made the Snowflake costume for Muffy to wear at a performance at MacVanderBearn Castle during their holiday in Scotland.

# Ornaments, Racks, Stands, Stickers, Signs

**ORNAMENTS**, 2nd series of resin holiday ornaments based on Family Holiday Collections: *Bal Masque, Red Flannel, Furrier and Ives, Musical Soiree, Nutcracker, Tree Trimming*, 2-1/2" to 3", boxed. *Ornaments are pictured on page 55.*

Boutique **CLOTHES RACKS** in white or stained wood finish, personalized, *at right*

VdeB **DISPLAY STANDS**, plastic: small, medium, large, with signature logo on front, *at right*

VanderBear Family **DOOR STICKER & STORE SIGN**, *at right*, "Classic Velvet"

**SPINNER DISPLAY**, "Life is one big dress up" turnstile with easel back, *at right*

# Muffy Rose

- Second Boxed Limited Edition of 10,000 for Club Members only
- Green satin body suit with rose petal sleeves and green ruffled collar
- Rose and green leaf petal taffeta over-skirt with a jeweled dew drop
- Gold ribbon rose trimmed slippers
- Flower pot hat with rose petals, ribbons, and a jeweled dew drop
- Gold personalized watering can
- Rose trellis display box with lattice-work doors and green ribbon tie
- Certificate of authenticity with Limited Edition number
- Factory Dressed only

*See title page for different view.*

# Holiday Sticker Book

30 stickers from 6 retired holiday collections. *Sticker Book is pictured on page 28.*

# Walking in Eggshells:
# The Egg Painting Collection

**Muffy:** white eggshell cap and play suit with pastel stripe pattern, miniature color swatch card on wrist

**Hoppy:** similar to Muffy's outfit with lavender background, swatch card on wrist

**Egg Decorating Kit:** oval tin with 3 wax crayons, paper egg collars, sheet of water transfers, stencils, All-Natural Egg Recipe Dyeing Book, hangtag, tin is 6-1/2" x 4-1/2" x 1-3/4"

**Egg Cups:** Muffy and Hoppy in hand-painted porcelain, personalized, boxed, Muffy is 2-1/4" x 3-1/2" and Hoppy is 2-1/4" x 4"

*Retired early because of difficulty with fabric.*

Shown at left: Muffy and Hoppy with Egg Decorating Kit, Egg Cups, and Egg Painting Collectors Eggs. Collectors Eggs are described below.

# Collectors Eggs

Hand-painted resin, inspired by old time sugar eggs, with Muffy and Hoppy posing in Easter Collections: *Muffy Bunny, Muffy Chick, Muffy Easter Fantasy, Hoppy Easter Fantasy, Muffy Egg Painting, Hoppy Egg Painting*, 3-1/2", boxed. (Muffy and Hoppy Egg Painting Collectors Eggs are *pictured above*.)

# The Queen of Hearts and the Bunny Knave

The classic nursery rhyme for a Valentine's Day Tea.

**Muffy:** polished cotton gown of love notes and candy hearts with eyelet neck ruff, golden crown**, red French court shoes

**Hoppy:** ruffle collared knave costume, red slippers, peppermint swirl hat, and the joker card under her arm

**Love Note Stationery Set:** royal fabric chest with 12 embossed love notes, 12 envelopes, 3 sticker sheets, 4 colored pencils, hangtag, 6-1/4" x 4-1/4" x 3-1/2"

**Rubber Stamp and Ink Pad:** heart-shaped, featuring Muffy, with red ink pad, packaged with header, 2-1/2" x 2-1/4"

*\*\*Crown is attached on factory dressed bear.*

> *Hangtag Note*
> *Envelope shaped in gold stripe, sealed with a heart. "Muffy VanderBear" is in white and "The Queen of Hearts" is in red.*

# 10th Anniversary
*This Takes The Cake*

- Boxed Limited Edition
- French blue taffeta gown with two-tiered scalloped skirt with golden swags, lace, pansies, yellow sash
- Black patent shoes with ribbon ties
- Crown of 10 "candles"
- Decorated gift box with certificate of authenticity on the side
- Factory Dressed only

*Hangtag Note*
*Round tag with pansy border. "Muffy VanderBear," "Tenth Anniversary" and "This Takes The Cake" are in purple and gold.*

**Muffy Trivia**
Muffy is 10 years old in people years; in bear years she is much younger. That way she never has to grow up!

# Beauty is Only Fur Deep:
# The Boudoir Collection

**Muffy:** cream cotton pique robe with monogrammed pocket, quilted collar and cuffs, insignia ribbon tie; quilted satin beauty mask; fur-trimmed satin slippers

**Muffy's Dressing Screen:** hinged wooden screen with striped fabric inserts, personalized flower motif, 11-7/8" x 8-5/8" x 3/8"

**Muffy's Vanity and Bench:** wood with adjustable, personalized mirror, two drawers, matching bench with striped cushion, 9-1/8" x 10" x 3-1/2"

**Muffy's Vanity Accessories:** frosted glass powder jar with silvery lid and powder puff, silvery hand mirror and brush, frosted glass atomizer for Muffy's pretend perfume "Furissimo," with antiqued relief images of Muffy as a Grecian Muse, boxed, 10-1/4" x 2-1/4" x 5-3/4"

# New Armoire Accessories

**Hat Boxes:** set of 3 (6-3/8", 5-1/2", and 4-3/8" in diameter) in pink custom print hat paper with VdeB ribbon handles

**Hangers:** 4 white plastic with pink Muffy cameo, 5", packaged with header

**Garment and Shoe Bag Set:** in custom print chintz, packaged with header, each is 7-1/2" long

**Boot Box:** custom boot print paper with 2 sliding compartments, 4-3/4" x 2" x 4-3/4"

*\*Hat boxes were retired Spring 1997.*

# Clubhouse Collection:
# What's The Secret Password?

**Fuzzy:** green carpenter's pants, beanie, suede sandals, T-shirt with "Dancing Hammer"

**Muffy:** periwinkle tie-on overalls with "Walking Clubhouse" logo, Jughead hat**, orange T-strap jelly sandals

**Hoppy:** yellow button rompers with "question mark", green T-strap jelly sandals, playhat

**Muffy's Secret Clubhouse:** wood grain cardboard with illustrations, boxed with instructions, assembled size is 15" x 10" x 8-1/2"

**Clubhouse Accessories:** wooden cigar box with secret treasures, contains list of rules inside cover, 2 decals, 40 original stamps, memo pad with logo, tin of 12 membership cards, 7" x 1-1/4" x 5"

**Hat is attached on factory dressed bear.*

**Muffy Trivia**
Muffy masterminded the Clubhouse, Hoppy drew the plans, and Fuzzy built it. The secret password has never been revealed!

# Rose Frame

Third renewal gift for 4th year Club members: hand painted resin, Muffy tending the roses, 7-1/2" x 6-1/2". *Frame is pictured on page 97.*

# Birthday Card II

From Muffy to Club members: Muffy "Flying Through". *Card is pictured on page 98.*

# Tricky Treat Trio

**Countess Muffula:** paper mâché mask, cape, bat motif pants, "M" dickey, fuchsia bow tie

**Hoppy Harecrow:** striped trousers, plaid patched shirt, burlap stuffing, burlap hat with crow

**Oatsie Oaterpillar:** caterpillar costume

**Tricky Treat Sticker Book:** pumpkin-shape with 32 original stickers

**Halloween Paper Decorations:** set of 3, Muffy, Hoppy, & Oatsie, with springy pleated tissue arms and legs, each 12" long, packaged with header

# Bathtime Collection
# Splish Splash

**Muffy:** hooded turquoise terry cloth robe and bear washmitt

**Hoppy:** hooded orange terry cloth robe and bunny washmitt

**Muffy's Bathtime Tub:** porcelain, aquatic illustrations, gold fish feet, 9" x 4" x 6", boxed

**Muffy's Bathtime Pitcher and Bowl:** illustrated porcelain set, pitcher 2-1/2"x 2-3/4", boxed

**Muffy's Bathtime Washstand:** wooden, marbleized backsplash with bas-relief illustrations, 5-3/4" x 6"x 4", boxed

**Muffy's Bathtime Towels:** 1 terry towel, 6-5/8" x 9-7/8", with Muffy and Hoppy appliqué; 2 face towels, 3-1/2" x 5", with "H" and "M" monograms packaged with header

*Hoppy retired Spring 1997.
Wash stand, pitcher and bowl retired
Fall 1997.*

69

# 1994

## Travel Trunk

Classic steamer trunk with telescoping hanger racks, one drawer, and one shelf; interior with printed paper of Muffy on her travels; faux leather exterior, metal corners, travel stickers, 7" x 11-1/2" x 6-5/8"

# 1994

## Figurines

Hand painted resin scenes, replicas of retired collections: ***Day in the Country, Sailor, Gibearny, High Tea, Safari***, 2-3/4"x 2-3/4", boxed, shown at left

# 1994

## Ornaments

Third group in series of resin holiday ornaments: ***10th Anniversary, Alpine, Snowflake, Muffy of the North***, 2-1/2" , boxed. *Ornaments are picture on page 55.*

# 1994

## Gallery

Resin frames with printed reproductions of past collections, each holds a 3" x 5" picture, boxed: ***Bal Masque, Musical Soirée, Nutcracker,*** *shown above top right.*

# 1994

## 10th Anniversary Pin

Hand painted resin, 2-1/4" x 2", packaged. Muffy Anniversary head with purple banner: "Muffy 10th Anniversary".

# 1994

## Retired Collection Tags

Special round hangtag indicates retired collections, gold with red border, Family tag is 2" diameter, Muffy/Hoppy tag is 1-1/2", *shown above top right.*

# Muffy of the North

- Holiday Boxed Limited Edition
- "Fur" trimmed Eskimo parka with seal motif on cuffs and hem
- Sueded mukluks and mittens detailed with Inuit-inspired designs (Inuit is the Eskimo's name for themselves.)
- Pet white seal tied to right arm
- Illustrated igloo-shaped box with certificate of authenticity on the back
- Factory Dressed only

*Hangtag Note*
*Blue and white tag with red border. "Muffy VanderBear" and "Muffy of the North" are printed in blue.*

**Muffy Trivia**
Muffy's pet seal was named I.M. Chilly through a contest in Fanfare.

# The North Pole Collection: Santa's Workshop

VanderBear Family Holiday trek to the North Pole to help Santa get ready for Christmas

**Cornelius:** Lapp-inspired folk costume, sueded boots, fleece hat, felt belt

**Alice:** folk dress with eyelet apron, tassel boots, traditional headdress

**Fluffy:** a baby doll in flowered corduroy dress, matching hat with felt wind-up key in back, white boots, paper baby doll mask

**Fuzzy:** sci-fi robot costume, square robot boots, antennaed helmet, paper mask

**Muffy Santa:** velveteen jacket, reindeer print pants, felt beard, plush trimmed hat, felt boots

**Hoppy Elf:** sueded lace-up jacket, polka dot pants, felt hat, striped socks, curled elf boots

**Lulu Reindeer:** antlers and harness

**Muffy's North Pole Sled:** natural wood, burned-in Lapp-land designs, medallion, ribbon lacing, 10" x 5" x 3-1/2"

**Muffy's Sack of Toys:** monogrammed felt bag with 4 embroidered toys inspired by Laplander folk art, 2-1/2" x 5" x 2-1/2", packaged with header

**Muffy's Trim-A-Tree Kit:** illustrated tin box that contains an 8" tree with wooden base, base cover, Muffy Santa tree topper, 12 original ornaments from the Collection with white ribbon, finished photograph, hangtag, tin box is 8-3/4" x 4-1/2" x 6-1/2"

**Muffy's Water Ball:** Muffy with Lulu and Sled, 3" x 4-1/2", boxed

**Wrapping Paper:** (30" x 20" sheets)
Reindeer Set with 2 sheets, 4 gift stickers, 2 paper ribbons, packaged
Muffy and Flower Set with 2 sheets, 4 gift cards, 2 paper ribbons, packaged

*\* Most pieces were still available into 1996, except for Muffy. Both factory dressed Muffy and Muffy outfit were sold out prior to their retirement announcement. North Pole was the first Lulu to retire.*

*Hangtag Note: Folded*

# Pajama Game

**Fluffy:** printed patchwork night dress with pink collar, monogrammed pocket, pink bear slippers

**Fuzzy:** patchwork pajamas with blue monogrammed pocket, blue bunny slippers

**Muffy:** striped pajamas, tasseled nightcap, pink bunny slippers, felt sheep on right wrist

**Hoppy:** checked pajama romper, blue bear slippers, felt and cotton kitten on left wrist

**Muffy's Night-stand:** wooden, monogrammed top, open shelf, 4" x 3-3/4" x 3-1/8",  boxed

**Muffy's Quilt:** pieced patchwork, pink thread ties, 13-1/2" x 11-1/2", packaged with header & illustrated insert

**Muffy's Lamp:** monogrammed base with 5 tiny sheep, paper shade with cut-out stars, battery operated, 4-1/2" x 3-1/8",  boxed

*\* Fluffy and Fuzzy were retired in Spring 1997, but Fuzzy was sold out before the end of 1996.*

✷*Variation:*

Later Muffys had lighter pink slippers.

# The Mozart Collection: One Minuet More

**Muffy Mozart:** moiré frock coat, stripe vest, breeches, lace jabot, plastic wig, French court shoes

**Hoppy Diva:** 18th C. taffeta dress, "Hoppy" in musical notes on bodice, gold shoes, tricorn hat

**Muffy Spinet:** 18th Century reproduction, "M" music rest, musical - Mozart's Zubearflotte (The Magic Flute), bench with moiré cushion matching Muffy's coat, 7" x 5" x 4-1/2"

**Muffy's Little Theatre:** cardboard Rococo stage and props, die cut, to assemble, 13" x 12" x 8-1/4", boxed

> *Hangtag Note:*
> *Hoppy first issued with "VanderBear" hangtag, corrected later to "VanderHare".*

# Birthday Card III

From Muffy to Club members: Muffy & Hoppy figures spelling Happy Birthday. *Card is pictured on page 98.*

# Fan Shape Box

4th renewal gift for 5th year Club members: pink and gold porcelain, black tassel, gift boxed with a thank you note from Muffy, 4-3/4" x 2-1/2". *Box is pictured on page 97.*

# Princess Muffy and the Pea

- Third Boxed Limited Edition of 15,000 for Club Members only, storybook role
- Elegant cotton nightdress with empire bodice decorated with pea blossoms, ribbons, and lace
- Attached golden crown with "emeralds"
- Illustrated canopy bed to assemble with 5 floral print mattresses, a tiny green "pea" sewn to the bottom, ladder
- Certificate of Authenticity and Limited Edition number
- Factory Dressed only

*Hangtag Note: Folded pea green tag with "Muffy VanderBear" in blue and "Princess Muffy and the Pea" printed in yellow. Story inside.*

# All Paws on Deck

VanderBear Family

**Cornelius:** cotton twill middy blouse, button-front sailor pants, sailor hat, espradrilles

**Alice:** twill middy dress with lace-up front and anchor buttons, straw sailor hat, espradrilles

**Fluffy:** old-fashioned bathing blouse with name on collar, pantaloons, bathing cap with bow

**Fuzzy:** old-fashioned bathing costume, plaid tie, "Float-A-Bear" water wings

**Muffy:** twill middy dress with red trim, anchor buttons, plaid tie, embroidered collar, black espradrilles, treasure map rolled into plastic tube on wrist that can be folded into hat

**Hoppy:** middy dress with black trim, treasure map, red espradrilles

**Lulu:** life preserver with "All Paws On Deck" motto

**Muffy's Boat, The Lulu:** wooden dingy, vellum paper sail, "Muffy" painted on the side, 16" x 6" x 14"

| **Muffy Trivia** The adventure takes place on Cornelius' new boat, Alice II. |
| --- |

# Bags, Balloons, Folders, Postcards, Buttons

**SHOPPING BAG**, triangular **GIFT BAG** (with tissue and tag), **FOLDER**, 18" **SIGN**, **BALLOON**, new logo **POSTCARD**, and new logo **BUTTON**. *Most items are pictured on page 98.*

# Brochure

Muffy's "Amazing Armoire" paper fold-out brochure with photos of Muffy and her wardrobe and a history of the VanderBears. *Brochure is pictured on page 98.*

# Checkmates

**Muffy:** lavender linen pinafore, acorn buttons, chess print bandanna, yellow flocked
   Mary Janes

**Hoppy:** orange linen pinafore, carrot buttons, chess print bandanna, blue flocked
   Mary Janes

**Chess Set:** modeled after all of Muffy and Hoppy's friends in decorative box with game
   board, 9" x 9", average chess piece is 1-5/8"

**Checkmate Chairs:** wooden bear chair, 7-1/2" x 5-1/2" x 4", and bunny chair,
   9" x 5-1/2" x 4"

**Checkmate Table:** wooden, carrot and acorn designs and drawer pulls, 9" x 9" x 4-1/4"

**Muffy Trivia**
Hoppy's pawns are carrots, representing clarity of
vision and thought. Muffy's pawns are acorns, sym-
bolizing the strength of the mighty oak.

# Czarina Muffina

- Traditional Russian costume from the Imperial era
- Korotenka (pearl buttoned challis overdress)
- Sarafan (underdress)
- Rubacha (cotton blouse)
- Koko shnik (velveteen head dress), "Muffy" embroidered backward and forward with gold and pearls

- Gold trimmed black velveteen boots
- Black velboa swan with red neck bow that ties to Czarina's korotenka

**Muffy Trivia:**
*Muffy and Hoppy's Magical Fairy Tale*
When Muffy offers the black swan her carrot, an amazing transformation takes place. The swan becomes her true bunny self — Hoppy Hopponova, freed from an evil spirit.

*Hangtag Note:
Accordion folded*

# Sleddin' and Skidaddlin': A Winter Frolic

New England Holiday in Bearmont

**Muffy:** Norwegian cardigan, tasseled cap, corduroy knickers, lace-up ski boots

**Hoppy:** crewneck sweater, tasseled cap, corduroy knickers, lace-up ski boots

**Lulu:** sweater with tasseled hood, outfit packaged on cardboard cutout of Lulu

**Skis and Poles:** wooden, decorated with Norwegian rosemaling, 8-1/4" x 1-1/4" skis, 6" poles

**Sled:** wooden, decorated with rosemaling, 9-1/2" x 3-1/2" x 1-1/4"

**Backpack, Scarf, and Mittens for Muffy and Hoppy:** each set contains a corduroy backpack with buckle, scarf, and mittens; Muffy's set is in rose and Hoppy's set is in plum; each set packaged as outfits only on cardboard cutouts

**Muffy Trivia**
Muffy's Sled belonged to Cornelius when he was a cub.

# Muffy Mouse

- Holiday Boxed Limited Edition
- Edwardian style suit with lace edged collar and cuffs, 2 yellow "cheesy" buttons at waist
- Whiskered rubber nose
- Pink tail with ribbon
- "Cheesy" lace-up slippers
- Personalized striped stocking
- Plate of cheese and crackers for Santa, dated 1995
- Illustrated book box inspired by the famous "Twas The Night Before Christmas" poem with certificate of authenticity on the back
- Factory Dressed only

*Hangtag Note:*
*Round tag with Muffy Mouse pictured. "Muffy Mouse" and "1995 Limited Edition" are printed in yellow.*

# New England Country Christmas

**1995-1997**\*

VanderBear Family Holiday at their rustic farmhouse in Bearmont

**Cornelius:** herringbone vest and trousers, band collared shirt, stenciled hanky, red velvety slippers

**Alice:** red sweater with grosgrain bows and monogram, lace cuffs, pleated plaid skirt tied with bows

**Fluffy:** plaid drop waist jumper, muslin blouse with ruffled collar, red slippers, plaid head bow

**Fuzzy:** herringbone knickers with suspenders, muslin shirt, red slippers

**Muffy:** lace trimmed green gingham dress, muslin pinafore tied at shoulders, satin bows\*\*, white felt boots, calico kitten (Purrlie) tied to her right sleeve

**Hoppy:** red gingham lace edged dress, muslin pinafore tied in back, felt boots, red and green ear bows

**Lulu:** stenciled muslin bib, yellow bow on her ear, outfit packaged on illustrated insert

**Muffy's Hot Chocolate Set:** 10 piece hand painted ceramic set, illustrated box

**Muffy's Country Christmas Table:** stained wood with original artwork, monogrammed, 11" x 8" x 5-3/4"

**Muffy's Country Christmas Chairs:** 2 monogrammed wooden chairs with gingham cushions, 4-1/2" x 3-1/2" x 7-1/2"

**Muffy's Country Christmas Cookie Tin:**\* 7 plastic cookie cutters and recipe card, hangtag, in 4" x 2" tin

*\*Cookie Tin sold out and retired in December 1995.*
*\*\*Bows are attached on factory dressed bear.*

# Paint The Town Red

A romantic Valentine night on the town, factory dressed only, Limited Numbered Edition of 4,500 each

**Cornelius:** red striped shirt, checked trousers, matching print bow tie and suspenders, two-tone spats, heart-shaped box of love tokens

**Alice:** red crushed velvet dress and cloche hat, monogrammed chiffon scarf, black handbag and shoes

*Hangtag Note:*
*Blue, red, and purple background with paint brush. "Paint The Town Red" is printed in black and white, and Cornelius or Alice's name is in white.*

# Hearts and Flowers

- Cherry red & white dress with lace heart bodice and a printed cross-stitched border
- Cotton batiste hanky with lace edge and embroidery, attached to skirt
- Red Mary Janes
- Organza headbow** with forget-me-nots

*\*\*Bow is attached on factory dressed bear.*

*Hangtag Note:*
*Round tag with cross-stitched heart. "Muffy VanderBear" is in black and "Hearts and Flowers" is printed in blue and red.*

# Spring Bonnets:
# The Silly Milly-nery Collection

Muffy, Hoppy, and Lulu make their own bonnets for the Easter Parade.

**Muffy:** drop-waist pink "hat print" dress with scalloped collar and spring bow, black patent Mary Janes, white socks, green felt up-side down bonnet with chick

**Hoppy:** green smock dress in "hat print" with eyelet collar, black patent Mary Janes, socks, red hat

**Lulu:** purple felt doggy bowl hat with bone

**\*Jewelry Tin:** kit with 9 Easter Collection charms, 6 blue eggs, green & pink cord, assembly suggestions, hangtag, 5-3/4" x 2-1/2" x 3/4". Tin illustrated with charms on top and the words "Trinkets and charms — Muffy's springtime jewelry kit."

*\*The Jewelry Tin retired unexpectedly in April 1996.*

> *Hangtag Note:*
> *Large tag with butterflies and flowers. "A Silly Milly-nery Collection" and "Spring Bonnets" are in green.*
> *"Muffy" is in red.*

# Cocoa Bunny

**Hoppy:** In chocolate velour bunny suit with purple satin ear lining, and purple trim, *first Hoppy issued by herself*

**Wheelbarrow:** Hand-painted, rustic wood with "Choco Loco Motion" on one side, "M & H Eggspress" on the other, filled with excelsior, 8-1/4" x 4-1/8"

*Hangtag Note Chocolate easter egg decorated with "Cocoa Bunny" in purple and "Hoppy VanderHare" in white.*

# The Reading Collection:
# A to Z by M. V. deB.

Muffy in alphabet print dress with her name spelled in buttons around her waist, felt slippers, tortoise-shell glasses with a ribbon to go around her neck

**ROCKER and CUSHION**, cream wood with tied cushion, embroidered with "Muffy", 7-1/4" x 5-1/4" x 5-1/4"

**Purrlie:** is all grown up with plaid neck bow, 4"

Purrlie's **BASKET & CUSHION**, wicker, name embroidered on cushion, packaged with header, 5-1/4" x 3-1/4" x 1-1/4"

*Hangtag Note*
*Muffy's coloring book: A to Z by McVdeB*

# Take A Hike:
# A Walk On The Wylde Side

**Cornelius:** barn jacket with "Take a Hike Society" patch, plaid shorts, moccasins

**Alice:** blue smock with red buttons, blue tam, moccasins

**Fluffy:** pink-print smock and tam, moccasins

**Fuzzy:** barn jacket with Society patch, plaid shorts, moccasins

**Muffy:** feather-print jacket with monogrammed snaps, Society patch, plaid shorts, ear-flapped hat, moccasins

**Hoppy:** gold thistle-print jacket with pewter snaps and Society patch, plaid shorts, hiking hat, moccasins

**Bench:** rustic wood with Society plaque, 11" x 6" x 3-1/4"

*Hangtag Note "Muffy's Sketchbook" is a 4 page tag bound with twine. It hangs around her neck, not on her waist as stated in the catalog. Hoppy's tag is a journal.*

**MUFFY VANDERBEAR CLUB KIT II** with new stickers, new stationery, and new Collection Album

**MUFFY STATIONERY & STICKERS**, with Muffy Butterfly and Rose: 10 sheets & envelopes, 1 sheet of stickers, for Club members only. *Both are pictured on page 98.*

**COLLECTION ALBUM** for new and renewing Club members: 2 ring, hard linen covered binder with new ribbon logo on the cover and picture inserts that will be updated, 8" x 8" x 2". *Album is pictured on page 98.*

# Muffy Pierrot
*First Collector's Edition*

- Limited Edition of 20,000*
- White velvet suit with black pompons and black trimmed ruffled collar
- Black satin hat and black satin slippers
- Mime mask on beribboned stick
- Marionette Pierrette bunny
- French puppet theater box, with certificate of authenticity on the back
- Factory dressed only

*\* First numbered limited edition available to non-club members, number is written on tag sewn onto bare Muffy. Sewn in labels mistakenly printed with club reference. See page 105.*

# Happy Birthday To YOU

**Muffy:** pastel taffeta check dress with lace-edged sleeves, petticoat, pink ribbon sash, pale pink Mary Janes, matching bow**, rolled party favor crown on her wrist, and a special card to send in and receive a gift from Muffy — a *Happy Birthday Magnet*!

**Hoppy:** pastel striped taffeta dress with lace-edged collar, petticoat, pale green Mary Janes, matching bow, party favor hat on her wrist, and a special card to send in and receive a gift from Muffy

**Lulu:** eyelet collar matching Muffy's petticoat, rolled party hat, outfit packaged with header

**Oatsie:** blue felt "Pin the Tail on the Donkey" costume, outfit packaged on cutout

**Birthday Party Set:** 4 decorated 2-1/4" plates, 3-1/8" cake stand, 4 monogrammed 2-3/4" spoons in birthday check box

**Tablecloth and Seat Cushions:** 12" x 16" cloth and 2 taffeta tie-back cushions to fit the New England Country Christmas Table and Chairs and 1997 Portrait Table and Chairs, packaging contains a birthday banner and placecards, packaged with header

**Cake:** resin, decorated in pink with "Happy Birthday To You," 1-1/2" x 2-1/2", boxed

*\*\*Bow is attached on factory dressed bears.*

*Hangtag Note*
*Oval tag with pastel check border and a birthday cake in the middle. "Muffy VanderBear" is in green and "Happy Birthday To You" is printed in blue.*

# Club T-Shirt

2 designs: (1) 5 lavender ribbon logo Muffys with "Muffy Club Charter Member Founded 1990" underneath, for charter members only and (2) a larger single Muffy Club ribbon logo for all Club members

# Birthday Card IV

From Muffy to Club members: Birthday Cake. *Card is pictured on page 98.*

# Cheerleading:
# Go...Go...Go Fur It!

**Muffy:** red corduroy skirt, white varsity cardigan sweater with "M", plaid bodysuit with white collar trimmed in red, headbow** with "Go Bears, Go Hares, Go Pups," saddle shoes

**Hoppy:** blue corduroy skirt, plaid bloomers, varsity V-neck sweater with "H", headbow and saddle shoes

**Lulu Mascot:** hooded sweater, outfit packaged on Lulu cutout

**Accessories:** felt pennant, megaphone, ribbon pompons, boxed with 4 cut-out trading cards on the back

*\*\*Bow is attached on factory dressed bear.*

*Hangtag Note Oval with red border. "Go...Go...Go Fur It!" is printed in red, yellow, and blue. "Cheerleading" and "Muffy VanderBear" is in blue.*

---

# Bare Muffy Hangtag

New folded hangtag with blue border was issued for undressed Muffys in Fall 1996

---

# Lulu

New oval hangtag with a border of bones, but same *Highland Fling* plaid bow

# Muffy The Red-Nosed ReinBear

- Holiday Boxed Limited Edition
- Brown Jumpsuit
- Separate hood with ears, antlers, and Rudolf-red pompon nose
- Mittens embroidered with "M" and Hoof slippers embroidered with holly motifs
- Decorated green felt goodie bag around her neck with a Santa doll inside
- Illustrated house box, with certificate of authenticity on the back
- Factory dressed only

**1996**

# Sleepshirt & T-Shirt

**SLEEPSHIRT** for adults with Muffy *Pajama Game* on the front, one size. **T-SHIRT** with single Muffy lavender ribbon logo, but without the words Club or Charter Member like the Club shirts described on *page 88*, available in adult and children's sizes

**1996**

# Muffy Mailer

Promotional brochure featuring current Muffy Collections, 6 page fold-out, 7-3/4" x 10-7/8"

# A Christmas Carol: Bearly In Tune

VanderBear Family Holiday, Christmas Caroling

**Cornelius:** woolly plaid double breasted coat with velvet collar, cuffs, covered buttons and pocket flaps; trousers to match; red satin ascot; spat boots; Hambearg style bowler

**Alice:** embroidered green velvet hooded cape trimmed in white "fur" and tied with checked ribbon, red satin underdress trimmed with white lace and ribbon at the neck, dark green sueded boots

**Fluffy:** velvet dress coat trimmed at collar and hem with white "fur", velvet hat, green sueded spat boots

**Fuzzy:** woolly plaid suit and cap with velvet collar, buttons, and pocket flaps; dark green velvet knickers; sueded shoes

**Muffy:** dark green embroidered velvet hooded cape trimmed with white "fur" and plaid bow, red satin underdress trimmed with white lace and ribbon, burgundy sueded spat boots with white trim and green buttons

**Hoppy:** velvet coat trimmed with white "fur" and embroidered capelet, embroidered velvet hat with plaid bow, sueded spat boots

**Lulu:** green velvet cape lined with red satin and ribboned tophat

**Oatsie:** embroidered woolly plaid horse blanket lined in satin, ribbon harness & blinders

**Muff and Reticule:** white "fur" muff with satin lining and cord, red embroidered bag with white tassel, packaged as a set in illustrated box

**Landau:** 18th century four-wheeled horse drawn carriage with raised seat for driver, working doors, bench seat, canopy that opens and closes, decorated with gold scrolling and "VdB" family crest, 22" x 12" x 8-3/4"

**Lantern:** "antique" embossed metal with bas reliefs of Muffy, Hoppy, and Lulu, batteries included, box is illustrated 1-5/8" x 1-5/8" x 3"

\* *The Christmas Carol Family members (Cornelius, Alice, Fluffy, and Fuzzy) were retired by North American Bear Co. in Spring 1997 but stock ran out Fall of 1996. Stores received their first orders and were able to reorder a small number of pieces until available stock was gone.*

✳*Variation:* Oatsie's outfit later changed to green velvet.

> *Hangtag Note*
> *Folded songbook tag with title:* ***A Christmas Carol***
> *Barely In Tune; SUNG BY Muffy VanderBear*

# The Messenger of Love

**Hoppy:** candy-striped overalls with embroidered scooter on the bib, blue high-top sneakers with embroidered hearts, messenger's cap, a blank letter (to be delivered to the Valentine of your choice) tucked inside her logo mail pouch, heart shaped hangtag

**Scooter:** red wooden "Hare-ly Davidson" scooter with carrot handle grips and hangtag

# A Salad Ballad: Waltz of the Vegetables

**Fluffy – the Gardener:** veggie print jumper with plush eggplant and carrot peaking out of the pocket, canvas gardening glove, canvas hat, woven tote bag

**Muffy – Queen of the Eggplants:** velvety eggplant costume with organza skirt, felt hat** with organza bow and ladybug embroidery, sueded dance shoes** with ribbon laces

**Hoppy – An Extra Ear-ly Carrot:** velvety carrot bodice with organza skirt, felt shoes with ribbon laces, felt leaf-trimmed carrot hat with organza bow

**Lulu – A Lulu of a Tomato:** velour tomato-red jumpsuit with stem adornment and felt hat, outfit packaged on cutout

**Purrlie – Purrfect Sweet Pea:** velvety peapod suit with pompon peas and stem, outfit packaged on cutout

**Watering Can and Gardening Tools:** resin eggplant rake and carrot spade, white tin watering can with vegetable decal, in gift box printed with cut-out "Seed Packets"

*Hangtag Note Seed packet cover with Muffy Eggplant.*

**Muffy's Apron & Tote Bag:** veggie print, packaged with header on cutout

**Benchbarrow:** green wooden wheel-barrow-shaped bench with Muffy and Hoppy cut-outs

**Grown-up Tote Bag:** canvas veggie pattern with "seed packet" pockets, 15" x 11" x 4", packaged with label

**Grown-up Apron:** cotton veggie pattern with "seed packet" pockets, packaged with label

*** Hat and shoes are attached on factory dressed bears*

# Square Dancing: Skip to My Lulu

**Muffy:** blue polkadot ric-rac trimmed bodysuit, tiered custom bandanna-print skirt with scalloped lace edging, red checked headbow**, little black flats

**Hoppy:** red checked buttoned-trimmed bodysuit with collar, tiered custom bandanna-print skirt with scalloped lace edging, red checked headbow, black flats

**Lulu:** tiered circle skirt and custom print bandanna

**Patti:** tie-back bandanna print vest, sueded boots (one pair)

**Square Dancing Accessories:** "Skip to My Lulu" print bandanna, straw hat with red checked tie, and sueded boots to fit Muffy, Hoppy, or Patti, packaged with header

*Muffy & Hoppy wear bodysuits, not blouses as stated in catalog.*

**Headbow is attached on factory dressed bear.*

> *Hangtag Note*
> *Country check print tag with "Square Dancing"*
> *and "Skip to My Lulu" at the top. "Muffy*
> *VanderBear" is printed across the bottom.*

# E.R., O.R. & R n' R: Mercy Me Hospital

**Head Nurse Muffy:** white pique cotton uniform with navy silk-screened hospital logo on the pocket and sleeve, stylish nurse's cap, white plastic shoes.

**Top Doc Hoppy M.D. x.y.z.:** cotton scrubs with navy silk-screened hospital logo on the back and on the pocket, green cotton surgical cap, white mask; operating room clogs.

**Lulu-Sick Pup:** white hospital gown with a navy silk-screened hospital logo; removable cast (signed by pals) for her paw.

**Doctor's Bag:** complete with eight bandage stickers, pretend gauze bandages, instructions on bandaging, and three lollipops.

**Ambulance** *(not shown)* **& Stretcher (shown):** painted wooden ambulance with handle and hangtag, detachable stretcher with Lulu outline.

> *Hangtag Note*
> *Plastic hospital photo ID card.*

## 1997 — Abra-CadaBeara: Hoppus Poke-Us

The Great Hoppus Poke-Us makes a special appearance in her first Collector's Edition of 10,000 individually numbered pieces. She arrives in her caravan, a collectible box complete with certificate of authenticity.

**Hoppus Poke-Us:** cloak is a satin cape with black tux underneath; tuxedo shirt and oxford cloth vest with silk-screened pattern of red and black cards; spats, matching wand and endless trick scarf

**Abra-CadaBeara:** a miniatured Muffionette wearing red dress and net cape with little hearts. Comes boxed in Hoppy's old world, gypsy-styled caravan. (Part of the Collector's Edtion, not sold separately.)

*Hangtag Note*
*"Hoppy's Book of Tricks."*

## 1997 — Portrait Table & Chairs, Sitting Pretty

Wooden table and 2 chairs with Muffy & Hoppy cutouts, same size as the New England Table & Chairs from 1995

## 1997-1997 — Birthday Card V

From Muffy to club members: Muffy Happy Birthday pop-out

## 1997 — Muffy Pouch

Renewal gift for club members, 5" x 7" plush zippered bag with coin purse and purple ribbon

# Puttering Around

Cornelius and Alice appear in a Numbered Limited Edition of 3,500 sets. They come boxed together, each with an individually numbered paw pad ribbon.

**Alice:** twill pleated skirt, red sweater with golfing bear motif, twill hat and red satin polka-dotted ribbon; brown and white golf shoes.

**Cornelius:** ivory twill knickers, red shirt, argyle knit seater vest with embroidered VdeB monogram; houndstooth check golfing cap; brown and white golf shoes; white canvas designer golf bag initialed with VB logo, a golf ball and tee, and three golf clubs.

# The Lemonade Stand: 5¢ a Glass

**Muffy:** pink pique pinafore that closes in back with a flower shaped button, lemon slice pockets; white pleated satin hat** with lemon floral trim; shoes—lemon yellow jellies

**Hoppy:** yellow trimmed tart green sundress; white pleated satin hat with lemon floral trim; shoes—lemon yellow jellies

**Purrlie:** wears a Sourpuss Café sandwich board; pink pique soda-jerk hat with lemon floral trim, factory dressed only

**Lemonade Stand & Paper Aprons:** Sourpuss Café lemonade stand, famous recipes featured on back; pad of twelve paper aprons and two ribbons, packaged with header, 8" x 10"

**Pitcher and Glasses:** frosted pitcher and set of four glasses with The Sourpuss Café logo in illustrated box

*\*\*Hat is attached on factory dressed bear*

> *Hangtag Note*
> *Folded lemon-shaped tag. Inside: "Muffy was here" and "Service with a smile!"*

# The Muffy VanderBear® Club

Muffy's Fan Club started in 1990 and now has over 22,000 members! Upon joining, members receive a Club Kit and a free gift each year when they renew. Through the years, a soft cover **Photo Album**, with all Muffy Collections pictured, was included in the Club Kit. This Photo Album has been updated three times and only the third one is still in print. In the first album, some of the dates were wrong, but these were later corrected.

**Soft Cover Photo Albums**
**#1 — 1990: Includes Collections through Spring 1991, cover with Muffy Gibearny & outfits**
**#2 — 1993: Includes Collections through Fall 1993, cover with Muffy and friends**
**#3 — 1995: Includes Collections through Fall 1995, cover with new Muffy ribbon logo**

In 1996, the soft cover album was replaced with a hard cover 2-ring canvas binder, called a **Collection Album**, featuring picture inserts. It is the gift for all new memberships starting in 1996 and renewing members in 1996 and is to be updated regularly. The 1996 New Membership Kit also includes a new set of **Muffy Stationery** that current members can purchase. Members have an opportunity to purchase extra gifts after the first year they are offered. The following chart lists all of the gifts that were included with memberships and renewals. We have included the price for those items presently available and the page number for a description.

| Date | Membership Gifts | Cost | Page |
|------|------------------|------|------|
| 1990 | Club Kit I, below left  (original price $12) | Retired | 36 |
| 1992 | Scarf/Bandana, below right | $8 | 51 |
| 1993 | Tote Bag, below right  (original price $9.50) | Retired | 59 |
| 1994 | Rose Frame, below right | $11 | 68 |
| 1995 | Fan Box, below right  (original price $10) | Retired | 74 |
| 1995 | Photo Album #3, soft cover | $4.50 | 97 |
| 1996 | Club Kit II | $25 | 86 |
| 1996 | Collection Album with Binder, *pictured on page 98* | $15 | 86 |
| 1996 | New Club Stationery & Stickers, *pictured on page 98* | $7.50 | 86 |
| 1997 | Muffy Pouch | — | 94 |

# Club Merchandise

In addition to the gifts that come with membership, Club members also have an opportunity to purchase other Club merchandise. The most popular of these are the exclusive limited edition Muffys. Members receive a redemption certificate for the Club Muffy and are required to place their order through a North American Bear dealer. So far there have been three of these special Muffys offered to members. A special surprise for 1996 was the first T-Shirt offered to Charter Members only.

| Date | Club Limited Edition Muffys | Page |
|------|------------------------------|------|
| 1991 | Muffy Butterfly, LE 10000 | 46 |
| 1993 | Muffy Rose, LE 10000 | 63 |
| 1995 | Princess and The Pea, LE 15000 | 75 |
| | | |
| | **Other Club Merchandise** | |
| 1996 | T-Shirt for Charter Members, only 4100 offered | 88 |
| 1996 | T-Shirt for all Club Members | 88 |
| | | |
| | **Birthday Cards** | |
| | Club Members also receive Birthday Cards | |
| | from Muffy, *shown at left.* | |
| 1993 | I. Accordion Fold-Out | 59 |
| 1994 | II. Muffy Flying | 68 |
| 1995 | III. Happy Birthday Figures | 74 |
| 1996 | IV. Birthday Cake | 88 |
| 1997 | V. Happy Birthday Muffy Pop-out | 94 |

### Other benefits from the Muffy Club:

♥ Three issues of *Fanfare* featuring stories and information about Muffy

♥ Three issues of the *North American Bear Newsletter*

♥ Pen Pals program

♥ Discount on North American Bear catalogs to keep you up-to-date on new collections

♥ Wanted & Fur Sale service for members to buy, sell, & trade retired Muffys

1996 Collection Binder, Stationery, and Stickers

Promotional Products — not part of club membership.

## MUFFY VANDERBEAR CLUB
401 N. Wabash, Suite 500
Chicago, IL 60611
1-800-682-3427

# Muffy VanderBear®: The Bare Facts

The following information is meant only as a guide for collectors. Based on our research, we have included dates when we think specific Muffys might have been made and a few examples of Muffys that came factory dressed on a bear with that tag. The tag samples show the front and the back of the tag and are printed exactly as they appear on the bears. Many collectors have contributed to the accuracy of this information, but there will be some variations and examples that may have been missed. We are aware that there were a few Muffys manufactured with a rare side tag, but have not included it in this guide. When we saw this tag several years ago, on a Christening Muffy, we were novice collectors and neglected to note the type of tag for future reference.

## #1 Tush Tag: 1984-1986, Korea

Muffy was born with a large looped tag on her tush, which later became known as the "Tush Tag" Muffy. Muffy herself was slightly under 7 inches tall with very short fur, tiny face features, small hips with legs fitted tightly together, and tan in color. The "Tush Tag" Muffy is the most sought after by collectors.

| | |
|---|---|
| VANDERBEAR FAMILY®™<br>©1982 ALL RIGHTS RESERVED<br>NORTH AMERICAN<br>BEAR CO., INC.<br>N.Y. CHICAGO 312/943-1061 | ALL NEW POLYESTER FILLING<br>SURFACE WASHABLE<br>MASS., OHIO, MAINE PA. (NY) 648<br>MADE IN KOREA<br>DESIGNED BY: BARBARA ISENBERG |

Actual Size (1-3/8" x 7/8")

Tush tag bears can be found factory dressed in:
**Christening I • Christening II • Cruisewear • Red Flannel**

Tush Tag Muffy, front and back.

## #2 Tiny Loop Tag: 1985-1987, Tag high on back, Korea

This Muffy was like the "Tush Tag" Muffy in height, but her fur was slightly longer and her hips were wider. Starting with this Muffy, the tags were placed high on the back.

*On some variations, the first line also has the trademark symbol: MUFFY VANDER BEARS®™

| | |
|---|---|
| MUFFY VANDERBEARS®<br>©1982 ALL RIGHTS RESERVED<br>NORTH AMERICAN<br>BEAR. CO., INC.<br>CHICAGO ILL 312-329-0020 | ALL NEW MATERIALS<br>STUFFED WITH 100% POLYESTER<br>MA, OHIO MEPA (NY) 648<br>MADE IN KOREA<br>DESIGNED BY BARBARA ISENBERG |

Approx. Size is 3/4" x 3/8"

Examples of some bears factory dressed with this tag:
**Christening I & II • Cruisewear • Day In The Country I • Nutcracker**
**Red Flannel • Taffeta • Valentine I • Witch**

Tush Tag on left, Tiny Loop on right.

## #3 Small Loop Tag: 1986-1989, Korea

During this period, Muffy began to grow. She was between 7-1/4 and 7-1/2 inches tall and similar to the Tiny Loop Tag Muffy, except that her fur was a little longer and plusher, resulting in a softer, shinier look.

Front and back views of #2 tiny Loop (on left), #3 Small Loop (center), and #4 Small Cut Loop (on right).

VANDER BEAR FAMILY®
©1982 NORTH AMERICAN
BEAR CO., INC.
CHICAGO IL 312/329-0020
ALL RIGHTS RESERVED
BARBARA ISENBERG DESIGNS
COSTUMES BY ODL BAUER

ALL NEW MATERIALS
STUFFED WITH 100% POLYESTER
MA, OHIO ME PA (NY) 648
MADE IN KOREA

Examples of some bears factory dressed with this tag:
**Black Cat with heavy glitter**
**Bunny with wicker basket • Cruisewear**
**Day In The Country • Furrier & Ives**
**Nutcracker • Out of it in Africa • Taffeta**
**Tree Trimming • Valentine I & II • Witch**

Approx. Size 1" x 1/2"

## #4 Small Cut Loop Tag: 1988-1990, Korea

Like the Small Loop Tag II, except that it was cut in two. By this time Muffy had grown to 7-1/2 inches tall, with even wider hips and legs that were set far apart. Her fur was the same as the Loop Tag Bear.

VANDERBEAR FAMILY®
©1982 NORTH AMERICAN
BEAR CO., INC.
CHICAGO IL 312/329-0020
ALL RIGHTS RESERVED
BARBARA ISENBERG DESIGNS
COSTUMES BY ODL BAUER

ALL NEW MATERIALS
STUFFED WITH 100% POLYESTER
MA, OHIO ME PA (NY) 648
MADE IN KOREA

Examples of some bears factory dressed with this tag:
**Angel • Black Cat • Tree Trimming**
**Christening III • Furrier & Ives • St. Patrick's**
**Valentine II • Valentine III, white**

Size varied between 3/4" x 1/2" and 7/8" x 1-1/2"

## #5 Small Cut Loop Tag II: 1989-1990, Korea

Like the previous Small Loop Tag II with a cute, small face and small ears.

MUFFY VANDERBEAR®
©1982 NORTH AMERICAN
BEAR CO., INC.
CHICAGO, IL 312/329-0020
ALL RIGHTS RESERVED
BARBARA ISENBERG DESIGNS
COSTUMES BY ODL BAUER

ALL NEW MATERIALS
100% POLYESTER STUFFING
SURFACE WASHABLE
REG. NO. PA. — 2865 (KR)
MADE IN KOREA

Examples of some bears factory dressed with this tag:
**St. Patrick's**
**Bunny**

Approx. Size is 1" x 1/2"

# #6  Long Single Tag: 1989-1992, Korea

At this time Muffy's fur took on a greenish cast when compared to the previous tan. She was still 7-1/2 inches tall, but with a larger chin and narrow face. Some collectors unflatteringly refer to this as a "doggy face." But don't tell Muffy!

#3 Small loop Muffy on left. #6 Long Single Tag Muffy from Korea on right.

Examples of some bears factory dressed with this tag:

| | |
|---|---|
| Alpine | Gibearny |
| Back to School | Gypsy |
| Ballet Recital | High Tea |
| Bal Masque | Musical Soiree |
| Beach | Out of it in Africa |
| Black Cat, glitter | Pilgrim |
| Chick, No black outline on eyes | Snow Bear |
| Cruisewear, snap & Velcro | Sweet Dreams |
| Day in the Country I & II | Tree Trimming |
| Down on the Farm | Valentine II |
| Dutch Treat | Valentine III, cream |
| Fir Tree | Wild West |

ALL NEW MATERIALS
100% POLYESTER STUFFING
SURFACE WASHABLE
REG. NO. PA. — 2865 (KR)
MADE IN KOREA
PLEASE REMOVE RIBBON, TAG
AND ALL TRIMMINGS BEFORE
GIVING TO SMALL CHILD

MUFFY VANDERBEAR®
©1982 NORTH AMERICAN
BEAR CO., INC.
CHICAGO, IL 312-329-0020
ALL RIGHTS RESERVED
BARBARA ISENBERG DESIGNS
COSTUMES BY ODL BAUER

Approx. Size is 1-1/4" x 1/2".

# #7  Long Single Tag II: 1991-1992, Indonesia

Muffy's fur and size were like the previous bear with the Long Single Tag, but she was made in Indonesia. These were made with both small and large chins.

#6 Long Single Tag Muffy from Korea on left.
#7 Long Single Tag II Muffy from Indonesia on right.

Examples of some bears factory dressed
with this tag:

Ballet Recital (some with "Cowlike" face)
Bal Masqué • Black Cat (glitter)
Beach • Christening IV • Gypsy
High Tea • Musical Soireé • Paw de Deux
Out Of It In Africa, Velcro
Yankee Doodle

MUFFY VANDERBEAR®
©1982 NORTH AMERICAN
BEAR CO., INC.
CHICAGO, IL 312/329-0020
ALL RIGHTS RESERVED
BARBARA ISENBERG DESIGNS
COSTUMES BY ODL BAUER

ALL NEW MATERIALS
100% POLYESTER STUFFING
SURFACE WASHABLE
REG. NO. PA. - 2865 (KR)
MADE IN INDONESIA
PLEASE REMOVE RIBBON, TAG
AND ALL TRIMMINGS BEFORE
GIVING TO SMALL CHILD

Approx. Size is 1-1/2" x 5/8"

## #8  Double Tag I: 1991-1993, Indonesia

This tag was the same as the single tag with an additional **second, wider tag** that included information on fiber content and a removal warning (in English on one side and French on the other). Muffy's fur and size were the same.

| | |
|---|---|
| MUFFY VANDERBEAR®<br>©1982 NORTH AMERICAN<br>BEAR CO., INC.<br>CHICAGO, IL 312/329-0020<br>ALL RIGHTS RESERVED<br>BARBARA ISENBERG DESIGNS<br>COSTUMES BY ODL BAUER | ALL NEW MATERIALS<br>100% POLYESTER STUFFING<br>SURFACE WASHABLE<br>REG. NO. PA. - 2865 (KR)<br>MADE IN INDONESIA<br>PLEASE REMOVE RIBBON, TAG<br>AND ALL TRIMMINGS BEFORE<br>GIVING TO SMALL CHILD |

Examples of some factory dressed with this tag:
**Bal Masque • Beach • Down on the Farm
Easter Fantasy • Gibearny • High Tea, Velcro
Mommy & Me • Musical Soireé
Out of it in Africa, Velcro • Paw De Deux
Sweet Dreams • Yankee Doodle**

Approx. Size is 1-1/2" x 5/8"

## #9  Double Tag II: 1991-1994, Indonesia

The narrow tag below was used again with the second wider tag described in #8. This tag is on **both the greenish/tan bear and the "new fur" Muffy** that came out in 1993 (more tan in color, similar to the older Muffy).
*There are also examples of this same tag from Korea. *On some examples the word "Polyester" is followed by "fiber".

| | |
|---|---|
| MUFFY VANDERBEAR®<br>©1982 NORTH AMERICAN<br>BEAR CO., INC.<br>CHICAGO, IL 312/329-0020<br>ALL RIGHTS RESERVED<br>BARBARA ISENBERG DESIGNS<br>COSTUMES BY ODL BAUER | ALL NEW MATERIALS<br>STUFFING: 100% POLYESTER<br>SURFACE WASHABLE<br>REG. NO. PA. - 2865 (KR)<br>MADE IN INDONESIA<br>NOT RECOMMENDED FOR<br>CHILDREN UNDER THREE YEARS<br>DUE TO SMALL PARTS & TRIM |

Examples of some bears factory dressed with this tag:
**Alpine • Back to School • Ballet Recital • Bal Masque • Beach
BeeKeeping • Black Cat • Bunny • Chick • Christening IV
Day in the Country • Down on the Farm • Dutch Treat
Easter Fantasy • Equestrienne • Flower Festival • Gibearny
GingerBear • Grand Tour • Gypsy • Highland Fling • High Tea
Kyoto • Mommy & Me • Musical Soireé • Out of it in Africa
Picnic • Pilgrim • Queen of Hearts • Rainy Day • St. Patrick's
Sewing Lesson • Snowflake • Sweet Dreams • Valentine II
Valentine III (cream) • Wild West • Yankee Doodle**

Approx. Size is 1-1/2" x 1/2"

## #10  Double Tag III: 1991-1993, Korea

Special tag for **Muffy Butterfly** has the edition number written in by hand. The back is blank.

| | | |
|---|---|---|
| MUFFY VANDERBEAR®<br>©1982 NORTH AMERICAN<br>BEAR CO., INC.<br>CHICAGO, IL 312/329-0020<br>ALL RIGHTS RESERVED<br>BARBARA ISENBERG DESIGNS<br>COSTUMES BY ODL BAUER | ALL NEW MATERIALS<br>100% POLYESTER STUFFING<br>SURFACE WASHABLE<br>REG. NO. PA 2865 (KR)<br>MADE IN KOREA<br>PLEASE REMOVE RIBBON, TAG<br>AND ALL TRIMMINGS BEFORE<br>GIVING TO A SMALL CHILD | MUFFY BUTTERFLY<br><br>LTD. ED._____ OF 10,000<br><br>MUFFY VANDERBEAR® CLUB<br><br>©1991 NORTH AMERICAN BEAR CO., INC. |

Approx. Size is 1-3/4" x 1/2"          Approx. Size is 1-1/4" x 3/4"

## #11  Double Tag IV: 1992-1995, China

This time the two tags were **exactly the same size**. The first tag was like the sample below. The second tag contained the same fiber information and warnings as previously described, except the words are printed in a different layout. These were all the "new fur" Muffys. Some feel that the faces on these were not as cute as the "new fur" Indonesian Muffys.

| | |
|---|---|
| MUFFY VANDERBEAR®<br>©1982 NORTH AMERICAN BEAR CO., INC.<br>Chicago, IL 312/329-0020<br>All Rights Reserved<br>Barbara Isenberg Designs<br>Costumes by Odl Bauer<br><br>TF 26-0392 | All new materials<br>Stuffing: 100% polyester fiber<br>Surface washable<br>Reg. No. PA 648<br>Made in China<br>Not recommended for children under three<br>years due to small parts & trim |

Examples of some bears factory dressed with this tag:
**Back to School • Ballet Recital • Bal Masque
Beach • Black Cat • Bunny
Cherry Pie • Dutch Treat • Equestrienne
Farm • Grand Tour • Highland Fling
Paw De Deux • Pilgrim**

Approx. Size is 1" x 3/4"

## #12  Single Tag: 1993, No Country Name

This special tag for **Muffy Rose** has the edition number written in by hand and is blank on the back.

MUFFY ROSE

Ltd. Ed._____ of 10,000

Muffy VanderBear® Club

©1993 North American Bear Co., Inc.

Approx. Size is 1-1/2" x 3/4"

## #13  Double Tag V: 1994-1996, Indonesia

These again are "new fur" Muffys. The second tag is shorter, but wider, with the same fiber content and warning information described originally.

*Left to right:*
#9 Double Tag II Muffy from Indonesia with old fur, on left.
#13 Double Tag V Muffy from Indonesia with new fur, center.
#11 Double Tag IV Muffy from China with new fur, on right.

MUFFY VANDERBEAR®
© 1982 NORTH AMERICAN BEAR CO., INC.
Chicago, IL 312/329-0020 - All Rights Reserved
Made in Indonesia • Barbara Isenberg Designs
Costumes by odl Bauer & Katya Bauer
This product meets or exceeds all government safety regulations. Not recommended for children under 3 years of age. If a child under 3 has access to this product, remove all tags, buttons, trim and accessories

All new materials
Stuffing: 100% polyester fiber
remove all trim before washing, Surface wash with cold water. Air-dry, brush gently if necessary
Reg. No. PA 2865 (KR)

Approx. Size is 1-3/4" x 3/4"

Examples of some bears factory dressed with this tag:
**All Paws • Anniversary • Bathtime • Beach • Boudoir • Bunny • Checkmates • Chick • Clubhouse • Countess Muffula Easter Fantasy • Flower Festival • Happy Birthday • Highland Fling • Mozart • Muffy of the North • North Pole/Santa Pajama Game • Paw de Deux • Pilgrim • Queen of Hearts • Rainy Day • Reading • ReinBear • St. Patrick's • Spring Bonnets Take a Hike • Valentine III, white • Egg Painting • Yankee Doodle • Sewing Lesson**

Both tags are exactly the same size with one as described below and the second with fiber information and warnings.

*Left to right:*
Original 6-3/4" Tush Tag Muffy on left and #14 new 7-1/2" Muffy on right

*Later versions of the tag below had the word water on the next line and the bottom number varied:
TF59-0594
TF58-0594
TF61-0594
TF24-0294

Examples of some bears factory dressed with this tag:
**Beach • Bunny • Cherry Pie • Christening IV
Czarina Muffina • Easter Fantasy
Fortune Teller • Kyoto • Pajama Game
Paw de Deux • Picnic • St. Patrick's
Sleddin' & Skidaddlin'**

*Left to right:*
The three different Muffy furs:
Original #3 on left, greenish fur #9
in center, new tan #14 on right.

All new materials
Stuffing: 100% polyester fiber
remove all trim before washing.
Surface wash with cold water.
Air-dry, brush gently if necessary.
Reg. No. PA 4345 (HK)

MUFFY VANDERBEAR®
© 1982 NORTH AMERICAN BEAR CO., INC.
Chicago, IL 312/329-0020 - All Rights Reserved
Made in China • Barbara Isenberg Designs
Costumes by Odl Bauer & Katya Bauer
This product meets or exceeds all government
safety regulations. Not recommended for
children under 3 years of age. If a child under
3 has access to this product, remove all tags,
buttons, trim and accessories
TF25-0294

Approx. Size is 1" x 3/4"

## #15 Triple Tag: 1995-1996, Indonesia

**Princess Muffy and the Pea** has 3 tags: (1) exactly like Indonesian tag #13 described earlier, (2) a shorter, wider tag with fiber information and warnings, (3) a special tag as described at right, with the edition number written in by hand.

> Princess Muffy
> and The Pea
> LTD. ED.____ of 15,000
> Muffy VanderBear® Club
> ©1995 North American Bear Co., Inc.

Approx. size is 1-1/2" x 3/4"

---

MUFFY VANDERBEAR®
© 1994 NORTH AMERICAN BEAR CO., INC.
Chicago, IL 312/329-0020
All Rights Reserved
Made in China
Barbara Isenberg Designs
Costumes by Odl Bauer

TF145-1193

All new materials
Stuffing: 100% polyester fiber
Machine wash, cool (in pillowcase)
mild detergent.
Tumble dry, low (in pillowcase).

This product is recommended for
all ages and meets or exceeds
all government safety regulations.

Approx. Size is 1" x 3/4"

## #16 Double Tag VII: 1995, China

Both tags are exactly the same size with one as described at left and the second with fiber information and warnings. *This was the first time that Muffy's tag has stated that she could be placed in the washing machine and dryer and that she was recommended for all ages.*

Examples of some bears factory dressed with this tag: **New England Country Christmas**

---

## #17 Double Tag VIII: 1995-1996, China

Both tags are exactly the same size with one as described at right and the second with fiber information and warnings.

Examples of some bears factory dressed
with this tag:

**Hearts & Flowers • Muffy Mouse • Spring Bonnets**

MUFFY VANDERBEAR®
© 1994 NORTH AMERICAN BEAR CO., INC.
Chicago, IL 312/329-0020
All Rights Reserved
Made in China
Barbara Isenberg Designs
Costumes by Odl Bauer

TF145-1193

All new materials
Stuffing: 100% polyester fiber
Remove all trim before washing.
Surface wash with cold water. Air-dry,
brush gently if necessary.
Reg. No. PA-4345 (HK)
Please remove ribbon, tags, and all
trimming before giving to a small child.

Approx. Size is 1" x 3/4"

---

MUFFY VANDERBEAR®
© 1982 NORTH AMERICAN BEAR CO., INC.
Chicago, IL 312/329-0020 — All Rights Reserved
Made in China
Costumes by Odl Bauer & Katya Bauer
This product meets or exceeds all government safety
regulations. Not recommended for children under
3 years of age. If a child under 3 has access to this
product, remove all tags, buttons, trim and accessories
TF118-1095

Approx. Size is 1-3/4" x 3/4"

## #18 Triple Tag: 1996, China

**Muffy Pierrot** has 3 tags: (1) as described below with her edition number written in by hand — Pierrot was not a Club bear, so the word Club is a mistake, (2) the regular tag with front and back described at left and below, (3) the usual tag with fiber information and warnings, not shown.

All new materials
Stuffing: 100% polyester fiber
Remove all trim before washing.
Surface wash with cold water.
Air-dry, brush gently if necessary.
Reg. No. PA-4345 (HK)

Approx.
Size is 1-
3/4" x 3/4"

Muffy Pierrot
Ltd. Ed.___ of 20,000
Muffy VanderBear® Club
©1996 North American Bear Co., Inc.

Approx. Size is 1-1/2" x 3/4"

---

## #19 Triple Tag: 1996, China

The first tag is as described at right. The remaining 2 tags are slightly larger and contain the fiber information. These 2 fiber information tags appear to have been one tag in the form of a loop that have been cut apart...the backs are blank.

Examples of some bears factory dressed with this tag:

**Cheerleading • Happy Birthday • Lemonade
Mercy Me • New England • Paw de Deux
Salad Ballad • Square Dance • Rainy Day**

MUFFY VANDERBEAR®
© 1982 NORTH AMERICAN BEAR CO., INC.
Chicago, IL 312/329-0020 • All Rights Reserved
Made in China • Barbara Isenberg Designs
Costumes by Odl Bauer & Katya Bauer
This product meets or exceeds all government safety
regulations. Not recommended for children under
3 years of age. If a child under 3 has access to this
product, remove all tags, buttons, trim and accessories
TF120-1095

All new materials
Stuffing: 100% polyester fiber
Remove all trim before washing.
Surface wash with cold water.
Air-dry, brush gently if necessary.
Reg. No. PA-4345 (HK)

Approx. Size is 1" x 3/4". *TF number varies.

# Muffy In The Spotlight

## Muffy's Golden Teddy Nominations And Awards

| Year | Nominated | Won? |
|------|-----------|------|
| 1990 | Fir Tree | Yea! |
| 1991 | Gypsy (Fortune Teller) | Yea! |
| 1992 | Dutch Treat | Yea! |
| 1993 | Kyoto Blossoms | Boo! |
| 1994 | Boudoir | Boo! |
| 1995 | All Paws On Deck | Boo! |
| 1996 | Happy Birthday | Boo! |

## VanderBear® Golden Teddy Awards

| | | |
|---|---|---|
| 1990 | Alice Musical Soiree | |

## TOBY® Nominations

| | |
|---|---|
| 1990 Back To School | 1994 Queen of Hearts |
| 1991 Wild West | 1995 All Paws On Deck |

## Collector's Choice Award

In 1995 Muffy was also nominated for a *Collector's Choice Award* in the category of Best Manufactured Teddy Bear! She was also First Runner Up in the Plush category of *Specialty Retailer Magazine's* Top Toys of 1995.

## Muffy On Paw-Rade

Muffy loves appearing in the Macy's Thanksgiving Day Parade!

| | | | |
|---|---|---|---|
| 1991 | Bal Masque | 1994 | Pilgrim |
| 1992 | Alpine | 1995 | New England Country |
| 1993 | Grand Tour | | Christmas with Purrlie |

# More Muffy® Trivia

**Special Bears**

There have been a few special VanderBears® that were made for a specific store or occasion. The most well-known of these is Garlee. Garlee was created in 1989 as an exclusive for Diana's Bear Den and the **Gilroy Garlic Festival** in California. This special white bear was made from the same pattern as Muffy® and wears a lilac princess costume with a banner that reads, *Gilroy Garlic Festival, 1989*. Limited to 2500, Garlee originally sold for $40. Although she is *not* considered a Muffy, by North American Bear Company, some collectors refer to Garlee as Muffy's cousin and she is quite collectible.

In 1991, there was a limited edition boxed set available only from **FAO Schwarz**. This was the same Muffy and Hoppy that appeared in all of the stores, but they were packaged in a special box. The set included dressed Muffy & Hoppy *Ballet Recital* with *Paw de Deux* outfits and was priced between $125 and $150. Neiman Marcus also had an exclusive Muffy set. In 1995 they featured Muffy *Grand Tour*, Lulu with her Tag and Leash, 4 Muffy outfits, and 4 Cameo Hangers all packaged in the Travel Trunk for a price of $198.

Fluffy and Fuzzy have also made special appearances in the past years. Fluffy *Day in the Country* was made for the **San Francisco Music Box Co.** with a music box in her tummy that plays the "Teddy Bears' Picnic" and Fuzzy got a real "kick" out of being dressed for the *World's Cup*.

## What Are Muffy's Charms?

Special Accessories that came in her pocket and were described as "Muffy's Charms" in the catalogs.

| | |
|---|---|
| Tree Trimming Gingerbread Cookie | 1989 |
| Gibearny Paint Tube | 1990 |

## The VanderBears Love To Travel!

| | | | |
|---|---|---|---|
| 1988 | Africa | 1993 | Scotland |
| 1990 | France | 1993 | Kyoto, Japan |
| 1991 | The Wild West | 1994 | The North Pole |
| 1992 | The Alps | 1995 | The Islands |

## VanderBear Firsts

1st Collection without Muffy — Classic Velvet, 1983
1st Muffy — Christening, 1984
1st Alice & Cornelius Alone — Remembearances, 1990
1st Hoppy — Back to School, 1990
1st Oatsie — Wild West, 1991
1st Lulu — Highland Fling, 1993
1st Purrlie — New England, 1995

## What Came As An "Outfit Only"?

Muffy and Hoppy Underthings, 1991
Muffy and Hoppy Back Packs, Scarves, & Mittens, 1995
Muffy's Salad Balad Apron & Tote, 1997

## Where Can You Find the VanderBears?

**VanderBear Manor:** Where the family lives most of the year
**Pawtucket:** New England location of their summer home, their favorite pastime is sailing
**Bearatoga:** Pony country near Pawtucket
**Bearkshires:** Location of "Aunt" Beartrice's farm
**MacVanderBearn Castle:** Originally known as Castle Wee Bairn in Scotland
**Bearmont:** Location of their rustic farmhouse

## Who Came Factory Dressed Only?

| | |
|---|---|
| Muffy Christening I | 1983 |
| Scottie VanderDog | 1989 |
| Oatsie Wild West | 1991 |
| Muffy's Farm Friends | 1992 |
| Bud & Rose | 1993 |
| Lulu Highland Fling | 1993 |
| Cornelius & Alice Paint the Town Red | 1996 |
| Purrlie Lemonade Stand | 1997 |
| Cornelius & Alice Puttering Around | 1997 |
| All Boxed Christmas and Limited Editions | |

## OOPS! Even Muffy makes mistakes!
### (But not very often.)

- Some of the dates in Muffy's first **Club Photo Album** were wrong, these were later corrected.
- The 1989 Catalog showed **Muffy Angel's** halo without stars...but all of the **Muffy Angels** came with stars on their halos.
- **Scottie VanderDog** is pictured in the 1989 catalog with a solid green bow, but it was plaid when he arrived. In the Spring 1990 catalog, the Scottie Dog is pictured with a leash, but it was never produced...perhaps because he ran away!
- The 1991 Catalog pictures Muffy **Wild West** with felt boots, but she appeared with red Mary Janes.
- **Mommy and Me\*** Wicker Setee and Chair cushions were in the blue teacup print, not solid as pictured in the catalog. *\*Note:* it was sold later with solid fabric and a teacup border.
- In 1992, the **Picnic Collection** is pictured in the catalog with a wicker **Picnic Basket** for Muffy. Unfortunately only a paper one was available.
- In the Fall of 1992, the catalog listed the **Pop-up Cards** with the inclusion of *Bal Masque*, but this was not part of the set.
- Muffy's and Hoppy's **Take a Hike** hangtags were around their necks, not on their wrists as stated in the 1996 catalog.
- The tag on the bare Muffy that comes factory dressed as **Pierrot** reads, "Muffy VanderBear® Club." Pierrot is not a Club bear; it is a LE for all collectors.

## Which Muffys have shoes?

| | | | | | |
|---|---|---|---|---|---|
| Nutcracker | Ballet Slippers | 1987 | Rose | Gold Slippers | 1993 |
| Furrier & Ives | Ice Skates | 1988 | Anniversary | Patent w/ties | 1994 |
| Tree Trimming | Mary Janes | 1989 | Queen of Hearts | French Court Shoes | 1994 |
| Valentine III | Mary Janes | 1990 | Boudoir | Slippers | 1994 |
| St. Patricks | Mary Janes | 1990 | Clubhouse | T-Strap Jellies | 1994 |
| Chick | Mary Janes | 1990 | North Pole | Felt Boots | 1994 |
| Gibearny | Mary Janes | 1990 | Muffy of the North | Mukluks | 1994 |
| Back to School | Mary Janes | 1990 | Pajama Game | Bunny Slippers | 1995 |
| Musical Soiree | Mary Janes | 1990 | Mozart | French Court Shoes | 1995 |
| Fir Tree | Satin Slippers | 1990 | All Paws On Deck | Espradrilles | 1995 |
| Mommy & Me | Mary Janes | 1991 | Checkmates | Flocked Mary Janes | 1995 |
| Wild West | Mary Janes | 1991 | Sleddin' & Skidaddlin" | Ski Boots | 1995 |
| Paw De Deux | Ballet Slippers | 1991 | New England | Felt Boots | 1995 |
| Fortune Teller Gypsy | Satin Slippers | 1991 | Czarina | Velveteen Boots | 1995 |
| Ballet Recital | Toeshoes | 1991 | Hearts & Flowers | Mary Janes | 1996 |
| Bal Masque | Laced Shoes | 1991 | Spring Bonnets | Mary Janes | 1996 |
| Butterfly | Velvet Slippers | 1991 | Reading | Felt Slippers | 1996 |
| Farm | Laced Shoes | 1992 | Take a Hike | Moccasins | 1996 |
| Dutch Treat | Wooden | 1992 | Happy Birthday | Mary Janes | 1996 |
| Yankee Doodle | Laced Shoes | 1992 | Pierrot | Satin Shoes | 1996 |
| Cherry Pie | Mary Jancs | 1992 | ReinBear | Hoof Slippers | 1996 |
| Rainy Day | Rain Boots | 1992 | Christmas Carol | Spat Boots | 1996 |
| Kyoto Blossoms | Accessory/Japanese Sandals | 1993 | Cheerleading | Saddle Shoes | 1996 |
| Beekeeping | Mary Janes | 1993 | Salad Ballad | Sueded Dance Shoes | 1997 |
| Sewing Lesson | T-Straps | 1993 | Square Dancing | Little Black Flats | 1997 |
| Equestrienne | Paddock Boots | 1993 | Mercy Me | Nursing Shoes | 1997 |
| Grand Tour | Velvet Mary Janes | 1993 | Lemonade | Yellow Jellies | 1997 |
| Highland Fling | Gillies | 1993 | | | |

# Special Editions At A Glance

## CHRISTMAS COLLECTIONS

| | |
|---|---|
| 1985 | Red Flannel |
| 1986 | Taffeta |
| 1987 | Nutcracker Suite |
| 1988 | Furrier and Ives |
| 1989 | Tree Trimming |
| 1990 | Musical Soirée |
| 1991 | Bal Masque |
| 1992 | Alpine |
| 1993 | Highland Fling |
| 1994 | North Pole |
| 1995 | New England Country Christmas |
| 1996 | Christmas Carol |

## BOXED CHRISTMAS MUFFYS

| | |
|---|---|
| 1989 | Angel |
| 1990 | Fir Tree |
| 1991 | SnowBear |
| 1992 | GingerBear |
| 1993 | Snowflake |
| 1994 | Muffy of The North |
| 1995 | Mouse |
| 1996 | ReinBear |

## BOXED SPECIAL EDITIONS

| | |
|---|---|
| 1991 | Butterfly, Club, 10,000 |
| 1993 | Rose, Club, 10,000 |
| 1994 | Anniversary, Muffy's 10th |
| 1995 | Princess and The Pea, Club, 15,000 |
| 1996 | Pierrot, 20,000 |
| 1997 | Hoppus Poke-Us, 10,000 |

## SPECIAL LIMITED EDITIONS

| | |
|---|---|
| 1996 | Paint The Town Red, 4500 |
| 1997 | Puttering Around, 3500 |

## MUFFY'S SPECIAL FRIENDS
### Accessory in Italics

| | |
|---|---|
| Scottie: | Tree Trimming |
| Lulu: | Highland Fling: *Bed, Brush, Bowl, Leash* |
| | North Pole |
| | All Paws On Deck |
| | Sleddin' & Skidaddlin' |
| | New England |
| | Spring Bonnets |
| | Happy Birthday |
| | Lulu with new hangtag |
| | Christmas Carol |
| | Cheerleading |
| | Salad Ballad |
| | Square Dancing |
| | Mercy Me |
| Oatsie: | Wild West |
| | Undressed |
| | Bal Masqué |
| | Alpine |
| | Flower Festival |
| | Equestrienne |
| | Tricky Treat |
| | Happy Birthday |
| | Christmas Carol |
| Purrlie: | New England |
| | Reading: *Basket & Cushion* |
| | Salad Ballad |
| | Lemonade Stand |
| Patti: | Down On The Farm |
| | Flower Festival |
| | Square Dancing |
| Mary, Webster, Rudy, Lucy: | |
| | Flower Festival |
| | Down On The Farm |
| Bud & Rose: | Flower Festival |
| Turkey: | Pilgrim |
| Seal: | Muffy of the North |
| Swan: | Czarina |

## CHRISTMAS ORNAMENTS

1992: Angel / Fir Tree / SnowBear / GingerBear
1993: Bal Masqué / Red Flannel / Furrier & Ives / Musical Soirée / Nutcracker / Tree Trimming
1994: Anniversary / Alpine / Snowflake / Muffy of the North

# North American Bear Company is always willing to answer collector's questions.

**Catalogs:** Older North American catalogs have become very collectible. There are over 34 catalogs and catalog supplements that include the VanderBears along with other North American Bear products. One unusual catalog is a box of 4 x 6 postcards with index tabs; in the VanderBear category there were 5 cards: the bare VanderBears, Black Velvet Family with Muffy Christening, Cruisewear Family, Taffeta Family, and Muffy Witch. In 1996 the VanderBears had their own catalog for the first time. Current and some recent catalogs can be purchased from North American Bear Company. Call for prices and availability.

**Missing Pieces:** If you are missing a hangtag or a piece from one of your Muffy outfits, North American Bear Company does have some extras available if the outfit is current or recently retired. Hangtags are free but there is a small charge for other items. Put your request in writing or call for information.

**The Muffy VanderBear® Club:** See pages 97 and 98.

**Tours:** North American Bear Co. conducts tours of their Chicago warehouse which includes their Muffy® display. Call their Public Relations Coordinator for information. The Design Studio in New York City is not open to the public.

North American Bear Co., 401 N. Wabash, Suite 500 • Chicago, IL 60611 • (312) 329-0020

# Muffy® In Print
Here are just a few of the places to look for Muffy.

# Books
Greene, Joan and Menten, Ted, *The Complete Book of Teddy Bears*, "North American Bear Co.," page 366, Publications International, 1989.
Hockenberry, Dee, *The Teddy Bear Companion*, "North American Muffy Bears," page 113, Cowles Magazines, Inc., 1995
Magnolis, Argie, *The Teddy Bear Sourcebook*, "North American Bear Co.," page 179, Betterway Books, 1995.
Menten, Ted, *The Joy of Teddy Bears,* "North American Bear Co.," pages 80-81, Publications International, LTD. 1991.
Michaud, Terry and Doris, *Contemporary Teddy Bear Price Guide*, "North American Bear Company," pages 133-135, Hobby House Press, 1992.
Mullins, Linda, *American Teddy Bear Encyclopedia*, "North American Bear Co.," pages 96-99, Hobby House Press, 1995.
Mullins, Linda, *4th Teddy Bear & Friends Price Guide*, "North American Bear Co.," pages 5, 20-24, Hobby House Press 1993.
Mullins, Linda, *Teddys Bears Past & Present, Volume II,* "North American Bear Co.," page 103, Hobby House Press 1991.
Pearson, Sue and Ayers, Dottie, *Teddy Bears*, "The North American Bear Co.," page 109, Macmillan, 1995.
Stanford, Maureen and O'Neill, Amanda, *The Teddy Bear Book*, "Collectable Bears Today," page 136-137, Simon & Schuster, 1994.
_____, *Best of Teddy Bear & Friends*, pages 83, 161, 162, Hobby House Press, 1992

# Magazines
"Back to School", Cover of *Teddy Bear & Friends*, October 1992.
"The Magic of Muffy," *Teddy Bear Review*, May/June 1992.
Michaud, Terry and Doris, "That Marvelous Muffy," *Toy Box*, Winter 1992
"Muffy Models Our Tailor Made Togs," Cover *Teddy Bear Review*, January/February 1995
Perry, Candy, "Muffy Mania," *Teddy Bear Times*, January/February 1996
Praytor, Shirley Vaughan, *Teddy Bear & Friends,* a regular feature article starting with the January/February 1995 issue

# Newsletters
Collins, Laura, Editor, *Bear Prints*, "Devoted to Muffy VanderBear & Friends," P.O. Box 824522, Dallas, TX 75382
Paw Pals, P.O. Box 66, Redwood City, CA 94064

# Newspapers
Tousignant, Mary Lou, "Wooing Collectors with Animal Charm and Magnetism," *Washington Post*, September 11, 1995.
"Costly Cubs," *Chicago Tribune*, November 14, 1994

# Glossary

**Boxed:** For this Guide we have included the box in the description only when the box is illustrated and it adds to the secondary value of the accessory.

**FD/Factory Dressed:** A plastic fastener is used to attach accessories to the bear. It is usually used for shoes, hats, or headbows, In this guide we have indicated factory dressed items on Muffy® only.

**Hangtag:** Special illustrated tags that come with every dressed bear, every outfit, and some accessories. Most of the hangtags will contain the name of the collection. They are usually hung around the neck of a dressed bear, but sometimes are tied to the wrist. The proper hangtag adds to the value of any retired piece.

**Header:** An illustrated heavy paper cover that is stapled over the plastic bag of most packaged outfits. If there is a hanger, it pokes through a precut slot in the header. Some headers on accessories have a hole for display hanging. Some of the older outfits that we frequently find without headers are the family Cruisewears. In 1996 some older headers were replaced with new headers, the collection name appeared on the front and new colors were used, example: *Pilgrim* and *Chrtistening.*

**Limited Edition:** Most collections described as limited editions, or LE, were lim-

ited to the time of production, not number of pieces. Only the 3 boxed Club Editions, *Muffy Pierrot*, Alice & Cornelius *Paint the Town Red, Puttering Around,* and *Hoppus Poke-Us* were numbered limited editions.

**MIB:** Mint In Box — in perfect new condition with hangtag and original box

**MIP:** Mint in Package — outfits with headers that are in perfect condition, have never been removed from the package, and with all pieces

**OF:** Outfit — most outfits came packaged with headers as described above. There is some discrepancy between collectors as to whether all of the older outfits came packaged with headbows. North American Bear Co. thinks that they did, but some collectors feel that they did not.

**Retired:** For the retired dates we use dates when the item was announced to be retired by NABCO. However, in many instances retired items may still have been available for dealers to reorder into the next year. Traditionally retirements are announced three times a year, in May, September, and December. In most cases family members of a Collection (Cornelius, Alice, Fluffy, and Fuzzy) are retired a few months before Muffy and Hoppy.

# Price Guide

It is difficult to print an accurate Price Guide for retired items, because values change so rapidly and vary in different parts of the country. This Price Guide contains a range of reported selling prices of retired VanderBears® based on our contacts in the secondary market during January 1997. Prices listed are for **factory dressed bears** only with hangtags and in mint condition. Accessories listed are also considered in <u>mint</u> condition with boxes if applicable. In the **ORP** column is the original suggested retail prices at the time of issue. In the **CV** column is the suggested retail price as of January 1997, or the secondary market value of retired items at that time. Retired items are indicated with an **R**.

| Collection | Pg | Muffy ORP | Muffy CV | Hoppy ORP | Hoppy CV | Family ORP | Family CV | Accessory ORP | Accessory CV |
|---|---|---|---|---|---|---|---|---|---|
| ALL PAWS ON DECK: Lulu / Rowboat | 76 | 38.50 | 40.50 | 39 | 41 | 284 | 302 | 15/64 | 16.50/68 |
| ALPINE - R | 53 | 35 | 50-75 | 35.50 | 50-60 | 280 | 300-450 | Oatsie: 28 | 30-40 |
| Sleigh / Tree - R | | | | | | | | 30/47 | 75-100 ea |
| ANGEL - R | 28 | 40 | 275-350 | | | | | | |
| ANNIVERSARY - R | 66 | 45 | 60-100 | | | | | | |
| Anniversary Pin | 70 | | | | | | | | 5 |
| ARMOIRE | 36 | | | | | | | 96 | 108 |
| Armoire Accessories I - R | 40 | | | | | | | 35 | 100-150 |
| Boot Box/Hanger Pack | 67 | | | | | | | 6.50 ea. | 7/7 |
| Garment & Shoe Bag / (Hat Box Set - R ) | 67 | | | | | | | 14 ea. | 15/15-20 |
| BACK TO SCHOOL - R | 32 | 31 | 50-100 | 31.50 | 45-60 | | | Desk: 22 | 125-200 |
| Watch/Notebook - R | | | | | | | | 36/9 | 50/20 |
| BALLET RECITAL - R | 43 | 35 | 50-75 | 35.50 | 50-75 | | | | |
| BAL MASQUE - R | 45 | 37 | 75-125 | 37.50 | 60-100 | 276 | 300-500 | Oatsie: 26 | 40-50 |
| Recaimer - R | | | | | | | | 380 | 450-700 |
| BARE BEARS: Tush Tag - R | 99 | 12 | 200-300 | | | 102 | 400-600 | | |
| Loop Tag - R | 99 | | 75-195 | | | | 350-500 | | |
| Current | | 17 | 20 | 17.50 | 20.50 | 135 | 165.50 | | |
| BATHTIME (Hoppy - R) | 69 | 33 | 35 | 33.50 | 35-40 | | | | |
| Towels / Tub / Washstand / (Pitcher - R) | | | | | | | | 7/29/23/12 | 9/31/25/15 |
| BEACH | 30 | 24 | 30 | | | | | 16 | 19 |
| BED | 36 | | | | | | | 60 | 60 |
| Bedding Accessories | 41 | | | | | | | 22 | 23 |
| BLACK CAT/Glitter - R | 20 | 23 | 75-125 | | | | | | |
| BLACK CAT/Stitched - R | | | 50-75 | | | | | | |
| BOUDOIR: Vanity / Screen / Access. | 67 | 35 | 37.50 | | | | | 50/28/37 | 55/30/39 |
| BUNNY (Wicker - R ) / Plastic | 23 | 25 | 40-50/33 | | | | | | |
| BUTTERFLY - R | 46 | 80 | 300-500 | | | | | | |
| CHECKMATES: Chess Set / Table /Chairs | 77 | 33 | 35 | 33.50 | 35.50 | | | 60/58/40 | 63/61/42 |
| CHEERLEADING: Lulu / Accessories | 89 | 38.50 | 40 | 39 | 40.50 | | | 18.50/18 | 18.50/19 |
| CHERRY PIE: Pie Safe / Cherry Pie | 49 | 35.50 | 39 | | | 88 | 101.50 | 32/5 | 36/6 |
| CHICK - R | 30 | 27 | 40-60 | | | | | | |
| CHRISTENING I - R | 11 | 18 | 400-600 | | | | | | |
| CHRISTENING II - R | | | 325-425 | | | | | | |
| CHRISTENING III - R | | | 250-350 | | | | | | |
| CHRISTENING IV | | | 29 | | | | | | |
| CHRISTMAS CAROL (Family - R) | 91 | 44 | 46 | 44.50 | 46.50 | 345 | 500-600 | | |
| Lulu / Oatsie | | | | | | | | 19/33.50 | 19/33.50 |
| Muff & Reticule | | | | | | | | 12 | 12 |
| Lantern / Landau | | | | | | | | 24/112 | 25/124 |
| CLASSIC VELVET - R | 10 | | | | | 144 | 600-850 | | |
| CLOTHES RACK | 63 | | | | | | | 15 | 15 |
| CLUBHOUSE: Clubhouse Kit/ Cigar box | 68 | 31 | 34 | 31.50 | 34.50 | 48 | 52 | 18/20 | 19/21 |
| CLUB: Kit I - R | 36 | | | | | | | 12 | 50-100 |
| Scarf / (Tote Bag - R) | 51/59 | | | | | | | 8/9.50 | 8/25 - 30 |
| Rose Frame / (Fan Box - R) | 68/74 | | | | | | | 11/10 | 11/10 |
| Soft Cover Album III | 97 | | | | | | | 4.50 | 4.50 |
| Kit II / New Stationery & Stickers | 86 | | | | | | | 25/7.50 | 25/7.50 |
| Muffy Pouch | 94 | | | | | | | – | – |
| COCOA BUNNY: Wheelbarrow | 84 | | | 38 | 40 | | | 20 | 21 |
| COLLECTORS EGGS | 64 | | | | | | | 13 | 6 |
| CRUISEWEAR/tush - R | 14 | 18.50 | 300-350 | | | 162 | Tush: 900 | | |
| CRUISEWEAR/snap - R | | | 125-175 | | | | High: 600 | | |
| CRUISEWEAR/velcro - R | | | 100-150 | | | | | | |
| CZARINA - R | 78 | 42 | 45-60 | | | | | | |
| DAY IN THE COUNTRY I - R | 17 | 19.50 | 100-175 | | | 175 | 500-700 | | |
| DAY IN THE COUNTRY II - R | | | 75-125 | | | | | | |
| DISPLAY: Acrylic Display - R | 22 | | | | | | | | – |

| Collection | Pg | Muffy | | Hoppy | | Family | | Accessory | |
|---|---|---|---|---|---|---|---|---|---|
| | | ORP | CV | ORP | CV | ORP | CV | ORP | CV |
| Boutique Header - **R** | 23 | | | | | | | | – |
| Display Stands: SM/MD/LG | 63 | | | | | | | | 2.50/4/7 |
| **DOWN ON THE FARM:** (Farm Cart - **R**) | 47 | 34 | 39 | | | | | Cart: 20 | 40-75 |
| Patti / Mary | | | | | | | | 20/12 | 21/12.50 |
| Rudy / Webster | | | | | | | | 11/8.50 | 11.50/9 |
| Lucy / Display Box | | | | | | | | 9/2.50 | 9.50/2.50 |
| **DUTCH TREAT - R** | 48 | 37 | 50-75 | 37.50 | 50-75 | | | | |
| **EASTER FANTASY - R** | 38 | 31.50 | 40-60 | 32 | 40-60 | | | | |
| **EGG PAINTING:** Paint Set / Egg Cups- **R** | 64 | 32 | 40-60 | 32.50 | 40-60 | | | 15/14 | 20/15-20 |
| **EQUESTRIENNE - R** | 59 | 37 | 40-60 | 37.50 | 40-60 | | | Oatsie: 29 | 30-50 |
| **E.R., O.R. & R n' R: MERCY ME HOSPITAL** | 93 | | 37 | | 37.50 | | | Lulu: 19 | |
| Bag / Ambulance & Stretcher | | | | | | | | | 19.50/32 |
| **FIGURINES** | 70 | | | | | | | 12 | 6 |
| **FIR TREE - R** | 36 | 44 | 400-600 | | | | | | |
| **FLOWER FESTIVAL - R** | 56 | 32.50 | 50-100 | 33 | 50-100 | | | | |
| Six Friends - **R** | | | | | | | | 91.50 | 100-150 |
| Garland - **R** | | | | | | | | 9 | 10-30 |
| Bud & Rose | | | | | | | | 9 ea. | 10 ea. |
| **FORTUNE TELLERS** | 42 | 36 | 41.50 | 36.50 | 42 | | | 26 | 26 |
| **FURRIER & IVES - R** | 21 | 28 | 375-500 | | | 221 | 600-800 | | |
| **GALLERY FRAMES** | 70 | | | | | | | 18 | 9 |
| **GIBEARNY:** Garden Bench - **R** | 31 | 31 | 50-90 | | | 228 | 400-500 | 96 | 250-350 |
| **GINGERBEAR - R** | 54 | 46 | 100-200 | | | | | | |
| **GRAND TOUR / TRAVEL:** Diary / Watch | 60 | 37 | 40 | | | | | 11/42 | 11.50/46 |
| **HANGER** - Plush - **R** | 18 | | | | | | | | 75-100 |
| **HAPPY BIRTHDAY** | 88 | 38 | 39 | 38.50 | 39.50 | | | | |
| Oatsie / Lulu | | | | | | | | 32.50/16 | 35/16.50 |
| Tablecloth Set / Party Set | | | | | | | | 17/15 | 18/15 |
| Cake | | | | | | | | 8.50 | 8.50 |
| **HEARTS & FLOWERS** | 82 | 35 | 37 | | | | | | |
| **HIGHLAND FLING - R** | 61 | 37 | 50-75 | 37.50 | 40-60 | 290 | 300-400 | | |
| Lulu - **R** | | | | | | | | 10.50 | 12-20 |
| Wreath - **R** | | | | | | | | 36 | 40-75 |
| Stocking - **R** | | | | | | | | 13 | 20-25 |
| Snowdome - **R** | | | | | | | | 60 | 80-100 |
| **HIGH TEA:** Chairs: Small / Large - **R** | 24 | 28 | 50-100 | | | 198 | 400-600 | 18/22 | 50-100 |
| **HOPPUS POKE-US**, 1997 LE | 94 | | | | 72 | | | | |
| **KYOTO BLOSSOMS - R** | 56 | 35.50 | 40-60 | 36 | 40-50 | | | 16 | 20-40 |
| **LEMONADE STAND** | 96 | | 34 | | 34.50 | | | | |
| Purrlie | | | | | | | | | 9.50 |
| Stand / Pitcher & Glasses | | | | | | | | | 10/19 |
| **LULU** | 60, 89 | | | | | | | 10.50 | 11.50 |
| Bed / Bowl | | | | | | | | 5.50/5 | 6/5 |
| Brush / Tag & Leash | | | | | | | | 5.50/5 | 5.50/5 |
| **MESSENGER OF LOVE:** Scooter | 92 | | | 39 | 40 | | | | 22 |
| **MOMMY & ME:** Wicker Furniture(3) - **R** | 37 | 31 | 50-100 | | | 68 | 100-150 | 89 | 150-250 |
| Tea Set / Frame - **R** | | | | | | | | 20/8 | 50/15 |
| **MOUSE - R** | 79 | 49.50 | 75-100 | | | | | | |
| **MOZART:** Spinet / Theatre Kit | 74 | 39.50 | 42 | 40 | 42.50 | | | 60/20 | 64/21 |
| **MUFFY MAIL & PAPER GOODS** | | | | | | | | | |
| Christmas Cards - **R** | 28 | | | | | | | 10.50 | 20-40 |
| Gift Enclosure / Greeting Card | 48 | | | | | | | | .70/1.50 |
| Holiday: Gift Tags / Pop-Up Cards / Stickers | 55 | | | | | | | | 4/5/3 |
| Holiday Sticker Book | 63 | | | | | | | | 4.50 |
| Stationery Set / Postcard Set | 48 | | | | | | | | 5/6 |
| Stationery Notecards - **R** | 33 | | | | | | | 4.50 | 20-40 |
| Sticker Book | 48 | | | | | | | | 2.50 |
| **MUFFY OF THE NORTH - R** | 71 | 49.50 | 75-100 | | | | | | |
| **MUSICAL SOIREE:** Chaise Lounge - **R** | 35 | 34 | 75-150 | | | 252 | 600-700 | 300 | 450-600 |
| Violin - **R** | | | | | | | | 12 | 125-200 |
| Tree - **R** | | | | | | | | 60 | 100-150 |
| **NEW ENGLAND CHRISTMAS - R** | 80 | 37 | 40-60 | 36 | 40-60 | 292 | 300-350 | Lulu: 14 | 15-20 |
| Table & Chairs - **R** | | | | | | | | 80 | 80-100 |
| Hot Chocolate Set - **R** | | | | | | | | 30 | 30-50 |
| Cookie Tin - **R** | | | | | | | | 14 | 50-100 |
| **NORTHPOLE/SANTA'S WORKSHOP - R** | 72 | 37.50 | 40-75 | 38 | 40-60 | 295.50 | 300-350 | Lulu: 15 | 20-25 |
| Dog Sled / Waterball - **R** | | | | | | | | 24/25 | 30 ea. |
| Wrapping Paper/ Santa Sack / Tree - **R** | | | | | | | | 5/16/34 | 5/30/40 |
| **NUTCRACKER - R** | 18 | 23.50 | 600-800 | | | 184 | 1000+ | | |

111

| Collection | Pg | Muffy ORP | Muffy CV | Hoppy ORP | Hoppy CV | Family ORP | Family CV | Accessory ORP | Accessory CV |
|---|---|---|---|---|---|---|---|---|---|
| **OATSIE — Bare** | 45 | | | | | | | 22 | 24 |
| **ORNAMENTS** | 55, 63, 70 | | | | | | | | 10 |
| **OUT OF IT IN AFRICA:** Rocker / Chair - **R** | 19 | 24 | 100-150 | | | 206 | 400-600 | | 100-150 |
| **PAINT THE TOWN RED -R** | 81 | | | | | 182 | 190-300 | | |
| **PAJAMA GAME** (Fluffy & Fuzzy - **R**) | 73 | 33 | 34 | 33.50 | 34.50 | 47 ea. | 50-100 ea. | | |
| Quilt / Lamp / Night Table | | | | | | | | 15/24/20 | 16/25/20 |
| **PAW DE DEUX** | 40 | 27 | 30 | 27.50 | 30.50 | | | | |
| **PICNIC - R** | 50 | 34 | 40-60 | | | 272 | 300-400 | | |
| Picnic Box set - **R** | | | | | | | | 24 | 50-75 |
| Tablecloth set - **R** | | | | | | | | 23 | 25-50 |
| **PIERROT - R** | 87 | 70 | 75-150 | | | | | | |
| **PILGRIM** | 25 | 28.50 | 38 | | | | | | |
| **PORTRAIT TABLE / PORTRAIT CHAIRS** | 94 | | | | | | | | 40/40 |
| **POSTERS - R** | 22 | | | | | | | 10 | 25-40 |
| **PRINCESS MUFFY & THE PEA** | 75 | 80 | 80 | | | | | | |
| **PROMOTIONAL** | | | | | | | | | |
| Bags: Shopping / Triangular | 76 | | | | | | | 1.10/4 | 1.10/2.50 |
| Balloon / Folder / Muffy Logo Sign | 76 | | | | | | | | .50/.40/17 |
| Button I / Postcard I | 43 | | | | | | | | .50/.20 |
| Button II / Postcard II | 76 | | | | | | | | .50/.20 |
| Muffy Spinner Sign | 63 | | | | | | | | 3.50 |
| VdB Door Sticker / Store Sign | 63 | | | | | | | | 1.50/2.50 |
| **PURRLIE / BASKET** | 85 | | | | | | | | 8/8 |
| **PUTTERING AROUND** | 95 | | | | | | 240 | | |
| **QUEEN OF HEARTS:** Stationery / Stamp | 65 | 38 | 41 | 38.50 | 41.50 | | | 22/13 | 23/13 |
| **RAINY DAY:** Umbrella / Puzzle | 51 | 34 | 38.50 | 34.50 | 39 | | | 8/9 | 9/9.50 |
| **READING:** Rocker | 85 | 34 | 36 | | | | | 36 | 38 |
| **RED FLANNEL - R** | 12 | 18 | 1000++ | | | 154 | 2000++ | | |
| **REINBEAR - R** | 90 | 49.50 | 50-75 | | | | | | |
| **REMBEARANCES - R** | 33 | | | | | 200 | 300-400 | | |
| **ROSE - R** | 63 | 80 | 200-300 | | | | | | |
| **ST. PATRICK'S** | 29 | 26.50 | 32.50 | | | | | | |
| **SALAD BALLAD** | 92 | | 38 | | 38.50 | | 57 | | |
| Lulu / Purrlie | | | | | | | | | 18.50/14 |
| Watering Can & Tools/Muffy's Apron & Tote | | | | | | | | | 21/14 |
| Benchbarrow / Adult Tote / Adult Apron | | | | | | | | | 29/32/35 |
| **SEWING LESSON:** Sewing Tin / Thimbles | 58 | 33 | 37 | 33.50 | 37.50 | 47 | 53.50 | 20/22 | 20/22 |
| **SLEDDIN' & SKIDADDLIN'** | 78 | 39.50 | 42 | 40 | 42.50 | | | Lulu: 17 | 18.50 |
| Back Pack Set / Skis & Poles / Sled | | | | | | | | 10/20/24 | 12/20/25 |
| **SNOWBEAR - R** | 44 | 46 | 150-250 | | | | | | |
| **SNOWFLAKE - R** | 62 | 49 | 75-150 | | | | | | |
| **SPRING BONNETS - R** | 83 | 37.50 | 40-60 | 38 | 40-60 | | | Lulu: 15.50 | 16 |
| Jewelry Tin - R | | | | | | | | 17 | 40-50 |
| **SQUARE DANCING:** Lulu / Patti / Access. | 93 | 36 | 37 | 36.50 | 37.50 | | | 17/29/21 | 17/30/22 |
| **SWEET DREAMS:** Muffy's Teddy - R | 34 | 30 | 75-150 | | | 192 | 400-500 | 5 | 40-50 |
| **T-SHIRT / SLEEPSHIRT** | 90 | | | | | | | 13/15-35 | |
| **TAFFETA - R** | 16 | 22 | 500-700 | | | 175 | 2000+ | | |
| **TAKE A HIKE** | 86 | 34 | 36 | 34.50 | 36.50 | 276 | 294 | 34 | 35 |
| **TREE TRIMMING - R** | 26-27 | 27.50 | 350-550 | | | 209 | 700-900 | | |
| Tree - **R** | | | | | | | | 46 | 400-700 |
| Scottie - **R** | | | | | | | | 9 | 150-250 |
| Cookie Plate - **R** | | | | | | | | 6 | 200-295 |
| Sofa -**R** | | | | | | | | 350 | 450-550 |
| **TRICKY TREAT - R** | 69 | 38.50 | 40-60 | 39 | 40-60 | | | | |
| Oatsie - **R** | | | | | | | | 32.50 | 40-50 |
| Sticker Book / Decorations - **R** | | | | | | | | 5/7.50 | 5/10 |
| **TRUNK I: STARS - R** | 25 | | | | | | | 28 | 175-250 |
| **TRUNK II: WHITE - R** | 25 | | | | | | | | 150-250 |
| **TRUNK III: MUFFY - R** | 25 | | | | | | | | 150-175 |
| **TRAVEL TRUNK** | 70 | | | | | | | 74 | 80 |
| **UNDERTHINGS** | 41 | 20 | 22 | 20 | 22 | | | | |
| **VALENTINE I - R** | 13 | 18 | 350-500 | | | | | | |
| **VALENTINE II - R** | 22 | 24.50 | 100-175 | | | | | | |
| **VALENTINE III - R** | 29 | 26 | 50-100 | | | | | | |
| **VdBEEKEEPING - R** | 57 | 32 | 40-50 | 32.50 | 40-50 | 247.50 | 250-350 | | |
| Honey Jars Lg. / Jar Sm. / Sticker Book - R | | | | | | | | 34/20/4.50 | 50/30/5 |
| **WILD WEST - R** | 39 | 36 | 50-75 | | | 257 | 275-400 | Oatsie: 24 | 50-75 |
| **WITCH - R** | 15 | 20 | 600-800 | | | | | | |
| **YANKEE DOODLE - R** | 52 | 35 | 75-150 | 35.50 | 50-100 | | | | |